D0929996

WITHDRAWN

Conversations with

I.M.Pei

Light is the Key

Everson Museum of Art, Syracuse, New York, 1961–64
Opposite: National Center for Atmospheric Research, Boulder, Colorado, 1961–67

National Gallery of Art, East Building, Washington, D.C., 1968–78

Morton H. Meyerson Symphony Center, Dallas, Texas, 1982 – 89
Opposite: Bank of China Tower, Hong Kong, 1982 – 89

Miho Museum, Shiga, Japan, 1991 – 97

Opposite, top: Grand Louvre, Phase I, Paris, France, 1983 – 89
Opposite, bottom: Grand Louvre, Phase II, Pyramide Inversée, Paris, France, 1990 – 93

Conversations with
I. M. Pei

Light is the Key

By
Gero von Boehm

Prestel

Munich · London · New York

CALVIN T. RYAN LIBRARY
U. OF NEBRASKA AT KEARNEY

Contents

Foreword

"Wherever you go, go with all your heart." When Ieoh Ming Pei first received this advice from his grandfather, he was perhaps eight years old. Today, at more than eighty years of age, he still lives by this maxim. His grandfather also gave him another important piece of advice, quoting Confucius: "If one day you are doing important things, always do them by means of virtue and you will be like the north star, which keeps its place while all other stars turn towards it."

There is one thing, at any rate, which the universe and I.M. Pei have in common: we know only a fraction of their true being. As far as the architect is concerned, this volume aims to change that. For the first time I.M. Pei—who prefers to be understood through his buildings and not through commentaries—speaks extensively and in detail about his work and his life, his influences and maxims, and the eternal search for perfection. Thus this book is also a kind of legacy dedicated to future generations of architects and, too, to all who live and work in his buildings, or who enter his buildings to contemplate art or listen to music.

Over the course of the five years during which our conversations took place (in New York, Paris, Berlin, Kyoto, and Luxembourg) and while we were working on a joint film project, I.M. Pei has become a wonderful friend. His buildings are a unique testament to how the convergence of two great traditions, the Asian and the European, can create new aesthetic standards—timelessness in stone and glass. But now we're already moving onto the tricky ground of interpretation for which I.M. Pei has little regard. Better, then, to let him speak for himself.

My gratitude for the generous assistance in the creation of this book goes not only to I.M. Pei himself, but also to Eileen Pei, Nancy Robinson, Shelley Ripley, Christine Reiß-Suckow, Victor Zbignew Orlewicz, Tim Culbert, and especially to Maria-Gaetana Matisse, who once upon a time brought us together.

Gero von Boehm
New York, June 2000

A 1920s portrait of the Pei family. I.M. Pei is seated at the far left; his grandfather is seated in the middle, and his mother is standing, holding one of I.M. Pei's brothers.

Family Roots

VON BOEHM: *Your roots in ancient China are very important to you—what do you know about those roots?*

PEI: The record of our family in Suzhou is six hundred years old. They were first mentioned during the Ming Dynasty, which lasted from 1368 to 1644. But before that our family came from the north, probably from Anhui Province. They came south and went to Zhejiang Province. Eventually one of my ancestors moved to Suzhou. Suzhou was then an important cultural center. My family were merchants of medical herbs, so I was told. They prospered, and became landowners of means. In Suzhou the family is remembered for its good works: they spread the money around and helped people who were not so well off. I must confess that my recollections of that part of my family history are rather vague, as my father left the family and went south to Canton and then to Hong Kong. I was not really exposed to the Suzhou environment until I was ten years old.

VON BOEHM: *What is your strongest memory of Suzhou at that time, when you were ten years old?*

PEI: In the mid 1920s my father moved from Hong Kong to Shanghai to be the manager of the Bank of China there. Shanghai is not too far from Suzhou. My grandfather insisted that I go to Suzhou in the summers because, as one of the oldest grandchildren, I needed to learn about the family affairs.

VON BOEHM: *And your grandfather himself was a symbol of the old China, which was on the verge of disappearing . . . We have to imagine the time: Five years before you were born, Puyi, the last Son of Heaven, had abdicated the throne, and China was struggling for a new order.*

PEI: Yes, but my grandfather, whose name was Li-tai, really represented the last generation of the old China. For me he was the very symbol of Confucian values. It seemed to me that his lifestyle was totally untouched by the West. He taught me the rituals of ancestral worship, with elaborate ceremonies in the temple-like ancestral hall located in the hills outside the city.

I spent several summers in Suzhou getting to know about many members of the Pei family other than my own immediate family. I remember particularly well playing with cousins of my age in the family garden known as Shizilin, the "Forest of Stone Lions."

VON BOEHM: *Is there a particular place you remember in that garden?*

PEI: The whole garden was of course an ideal playground for us. I found that the caves in the rocks, the stone bridges, the ponds and waterfalls, were most stimulating to our fantasies.

Chinese gardens are just the opposite of French gardens. They are designed for painters and poets and not for princes and kings. The Forest of Stone Lions was started by a Taoist monk in the fourteenth century, and is famous for its rocks, which look rather like the works of Dubuffet. How such rock gardens are made is very interesting, and refers strongly to our perception of time and family relationships. The rock is usually a porous volcanic stone, which is chosen by a rock farmer for its sculptural possibilities. The rock farmer would carefully chisel the rock to open it up in a subtle way. Then the rock farmer would carefully select a spot near the edge of a lake or a river, with moving water, and would plant the rock there to erode in a natural way over a generation, or several generations. The farmer himself, or his son or grandson, would later harvest the rock, and incorporate it into the composition of a garden. This sense of connection, of continuity, is an extremely telling aspect of Chinese culture—the father sows, and the son will reap.

VON BOEHM: *Is it the sense of connection with the past, the sense of continuity, that fascinates you so much?*

PEI: Yes. Man creates to complement nature, and nature has its effects on man's creations. My own work is very much in that spirit. The shapes of my buildings are chosen most carefully, and placed most carefully in response to the functional currents swirling around them. And the process of architecture itself must be responsive to different clients, different cultures, governments, the pull of economics. Sometimes the process stops because of some difficulty and then—after years—goes on again. From the beginning of a design idea, through construction, to the completed building, takes many years. The process often reminds me of rock farming.

Shizilin garden

VON BOEHM: *When one looks at the perspectives, at the atriums and courtyards in the garden of your childhood and at the family palace in this garden, the early influence becomes quite clear. To me it is obvious.*

PEI: I was not aware that I learned anything from my experiences in Suzhou until much later. When I think about it in retrospect I must say that, yes, it did have an influence on my work. It made me aware of the complimentarity of man and nature, not of just nature alone. Somehow, the hand of man joined with nature becomes the essence of creativity. The gardens of Suzhou taught me that lesson.

VON BOEHM: *If you look at the moon gates in that garden, for instance—you find them in your architecture much later, again and again.*

PEI: Really? Maybe . . . that is interesting. I think you are right. The circular form is a beautiful form. It is commonly used in Chinese gardens to frame a vista. I used it as an entrance to the Miho Museum in Kyoto. But this is not the only thing I learned—there were many others. Most importantly, I learned about the meaning of family, its cohesiveness, and its history.

VON BOEHM: *Are they important to you?*

PEI: They are important to me now. When I was in Hong Kong as a child, I was never aware of that. My family consisted only of my father and mother and my siblings. There we were transplanted. But after I returned to Suzhou, I realized that I came from much deeper roots. That was a revelation, and has had considerable influence on me. I must really say that as I look back now.

VON BOEHM: *Can you define that influence?*

PEI: It does affect my philosophy of life, relationships with people. I am much more sensitive to that than if I hadn't been to Suzhou because that is an old world . . . an old society where people treat each other with thoughtfulness and respect. The relationships between people were much more important in one's daily life in Suzhou then. And that's what life is all about—don't you think so? I have come to appreciate the important relationship between life and architecture.

VON BOEHM: *You mean that you could never separate life from architecture because architecture is your life? That is certainly true of all the professions where you need a lot of creativity and passion.*

The Shanghai Years
and Early Influences

VON BOEHM: *When did you first see the buildings of Shanghai and what was your first impression? At the time, you certainly weren't thinking much about architecture.*

PEI: I went there after Hong Kong so it was not that much of a shock. I was about ten years old. Shanghai was much more advanced than Hong Kong at that time. Shanghai was really *the* metropolis in Asia. I was told it was the Paris of the Orient. Very interesting. Shanghai in the twenties was a city of tremendous vitality, partly due to the many foreign concessions which made it a cosmopolitan center in the Far East.

VON BOEHM: *People liked to call it the "Paris of the East" at the time—also because literature and the arts, music and dance played an important role. What do you remember of that?*

PEI: The city was very international in character and therefore open-minded and tolerant. I attended school there, and obviously because of the influx of modern ideas that came to Shanghai I took a certain profit from it. I was exposed to the new in architecture and the arts, but also in lifestyle. It was a very exciting, but also a very corrupt place. So I learned both good and bad from Shanghai. The good part of it was that I saw a little of the future in Shanghai that I was not able to see in Suzhou. In Suzhou I was very much conscious of the past, but in Shanghai I saw the future or the beginning of the future. The new buildings that went up in Shanghai obviously had an influence on me. I was quite taken, as a matter of fact, that they were able to build taller and taller buildings. That was very unusual. In Suzhou we had only one, two or three story buildings and that was all, but in Shanghai they were building ten, twenty and thirty stories. So I became interested in architecture, largely because of that.

VON BOEHM: *Especially when you looked at the ensemble of the buildings at the Bund, the elegant promenade on the river shore, I suppose.*

PEI: Yes, nobody could escape that impression. It was very strong. Nevertheless the Bund was still a bit of the past for me. The future was not in the Bund. The Bund was still very much a colonial past. The new building happened in midtown and not in downtown. Midtown, that is where all the new buildings were constructed. The Park Hotel, for instance. At the time, it was my favorite building. It was the tallest building in the Far East and it was lavish and glamorous—meaning Western glamour, of course. The hotel was twenty-six stories high, it contained more than 200 rooms, equipped with the utmost luxury of that time.

The Shanghai waterfront in the 1930s

VON BOEHM: *Did you know then who the architect was? Were you interested in details like that?*

PEI: Of course I informed myself and found out that it was an architect from Czechoslovakia by the name of Ladislav Hudek. He was actually the master of colonial classicism, which was typical for Shanghai at the time. There I could already see the clear lines of a new style arising in the West. And how high that building was—the idea of height alone fascinated me immensely and it was then that I decided that what I wanted to do was design buildings. But there were also other attractions in Shanghai. I used to spend my weekends going to theaters nearby and I loved to play billiards. Now that might sound strange to you, but that was a form of amusement for young people in China at that time. I became quite a good billiard player. While I was playing billiards and going to the cinema, this building was going up, getting taller and taller. It became twenty-four stories high. That had an influence on me and gave me a glimpse into the future. I owe that to Shanghai.

VON BOEHM: *As Louis Kahn once said, "A city is a place where a small boy, as he walks through it, may see something that will tell him what he wants to do his whole life." But let's talk for a moment about billiards: Did you like to play billiards because of the geometry in this game?*

PEI: Yes, I suppose so. Billiards is a game of geometry. I played it, I was quite good at it. It's really the vector, it's really a question of geometric vectors. By playing billiards you can have an understanding about geometry, something I only became aware of afterwards. And billiards is also a strategic game. Some of the elements you need as an architect come together in billiards, that is very true.

VON BOEHM: *Even all that has to do with tradition. I would very much like to know which values were very important to your grandparents and to your parents. Tell me a little bit more about how they passed these values on to you and the environment in which you grew up.*

PEI: I was brought up in a typical Chinese family living in Shanghai. It was actually not at all cosmopolitan. It was a very traditional family. Therefore, the Chinese values were very much ingrained in me when I was a young man. In fact my grandfather was so insistent that I learn more about the so-called Chinese values that exactly this was the reason why he invited me to stay with him in Suzhou. It sort of made me feel tied to the long line of ancestors. In other words, the Confucian values were pretty much my upbringing. Of course, I had the other side in my early life when I lived in Hong Kong with my family because my father was banker there. I was able to see a little bit of the West. The upbringing was absolutely Chinese.

VON BOEHM: *Which Confucian values were you actually taught? Which ones were considered to be very important? For Westerners, it may not be obvious which values you mean, and "Confucian values" may be a very vague idea for us.*

PEI: For us I think it is also a very vague concept. Of course there is the very important hierarchy of relationships. There is the King, the Ministers, the Father, the Son, husband and wife, brothers and friends. You see, values in life, ethical values, are based on this hierarchy of respect. I was brought up with that. When I was young, there was no emperor and the revolution had already taken place. But the Confucian ethics remained very central in my earlier upbringing.

VON BOEHM: *Can this tradition, and tradition in general, be a good base for a certain freedom because you don't have to think about certain things in life anymore? They become natural, and this can give you freedom to think about other things. That is how I see tradition.*

PEI: I absolutely see it the same way, if we talk about tradition in general—the principal idea you just developed is also true for architecture by the way. But let me say something more about Chinese tradition—it is a good example and nevertheless a special case.

I can only speak for my generation. You see, the Confucian values had underpinned Chinese society for twenty-five hundred years. I'm not saying it has disappeared from China; it has not. It will continue. But when I came along, the emphasis had lessened. It was not as strong as it was in my father's time, or my grandfather's time. Did that give me greater freedom? Yes, in the following sense: the relationship between men is very important in our tradition. To receive and to give . . . I am translating Chinese now . . . is a way of life. One has to know how to receive and how to give. I was taught that when I was very young. Confucian ethics is in some ways a very pragmatic philosophy. It is not a religion. I think the West sometimes tends to confuse that. It is not a religion; it is a way of acting and behaving in the world. It is the same as ethical relationships. It is not a religion at all.

VON BOEHM: *That's what I think. These rules make things easier because certain conditions are already clear. You don't have to discuss much. Within this framework you will gain some freedom.*

PEI: I do see it the same way. At the same time, I think there is a major difference between China and the West. I think religion is very central to Westerners. I think belief in God, which is something I cannot talk about with conviction, does give you not a certain boundary or limitation, but an impetus to act because of an abstract belief in something. That I find is not in my upbringing. I don't know how having that would have affected my life. But I do believe there is a similarity between Confucius' teaching and the Sermon on the Mount. He is not the only sage. There were others— Mencius, Lao-tse, and many others—who combine to form a philosophic basis for so-called Chinese society. That religious element is absent in my life. I would very much like to know what kind of person I would have become if I had had that. I often wonder.

VON BOEHM: *Do you think you missed something by not having it—this ability to believe?*

PEI: Yes, in a way I missed it. Think of the wonderful things that were created for the glorification of God. Think of it. Think of all the great works that have been done—in the arts, in music and in architecture. It is that inspiration that is something I cannot estimate, nor do I know how much I have missed. It is difficult for me to tell. As far as in my life . . . ethical behavior in my life . . . I think I would have behaved the same way, exactly the same way were I a Christian or a Buddhist.

VON BOEHM: *Your mother was a Buddhist, a practicing Buddhist.*

PEI: Yes, she was a devout Buddhist and I remember her taking me with her to one of her regular retreats in a monastery. I had to sit there over long periods in silent meditation. That is among the things my mother taught me: to listen to the silence.

VON BOEHM: *When your mother died you were only thirteen.*

PEI: Yes, I was just turning thirteen. I was grief stricken. I can say this without my sisters and brothers contradicting me. I think that her death affected me more than the others because I was of that age when I was becoming aware of the importance of the mother. I am not saying that it was not the case for my younger brothers, but I think it certainly was for me. I was the one who was called to her deathbed. And I had been given the honor of preparing for her the long-stemmed opium pipe. She needed opium because of the pain she suffered from—she died of cancer. The last thing she told me was to take care of my brothers and sisters and to set an example. She was very important to me.

VON BOEHM: *She obviously was an enormous influence on you in your early childhood. Can you define that influence?*

PEI: I think the way she acted and the way she lived her life was the example that influenced me a lot. She was very popular with her friends. She had many friends. That impressed me. They would say so-and-so's aunt is coming, and they got together and they talked. I was privileged enough to listen to those conversations. I sensed that there was a great deal of friendship, deep friendship between them and among them. That I think gives you a sense, a certain judgment about my mother as a human being. She must have been extremely warm as a person and people respected her. That has influenced me.

VON BOEHM: *When your mother died you were not only deprived of her, which was very hard for you, but also of your family home as well . . .*

PEI: . . . because my father could no longer personally take care of us. He left my brothers and sisters and myself in the care of family retainers. We grew up under their care. My father began living his own separate life pretty soon after that. He was a very busy man. Our home was no longer a home. My father did not wish us to remain in the house, so he found a very large apartment for my sisters and brothers to live in. From that point on my father and we actually lived separate lives. I lived that life without a mother for about three or four years. My father was rather depressed after the death of my mother. The Bank's board persuaded him to take a trip abroad. That is when he met my stepmother. Her father was a deputy ambassador of China to Italy. They were married soon afterwards.

The Influence of Music

VON BOEHM: *You like to compare architecture with music—what do both have in common, and what kind of music made a mark on you when you were young?*

PEI: In China, we didn't know much about Western music. My first experience with it was at the symphony hall in Boston, which is one of the finest concert halls in the United States. I was deeply moved by the performance, which was one of Beethoven's symphonies. From that point on I spent a lot of time in music stores, buying records—I built up quite a large collection. Later I gave most of them away to friends who collected them as antiques.

VON BOEHM: *Was it emotion that you felt or was it also something a little bit more analytic . . . experiencing this music?*

PEI: It was between the two really. There had to be an emotional reaction first, but it just seemed right to my ears. I knew Chinese music. My mother was a flutist. Western classical music was new for me, strange as it may seem. In Shanghai I knew jazz music, but that is not classical music. So when I was first exposed to Beethoven, Mozart, Bach, and Schubert, it was all new to me, and I took to it just like a fish takes to water. Even today, sixty-some years later, it is still my passion to listen to that kind of music.

VON BOEHM: *When you work do you listen to music?*

PEI: Yes, certain kinds. Piano music is usually my choice.

VON BOEHM: *What is the best music for working and what is the best music for meditation?*

PEI: That is a very good question. I cannot work and listen to Wagner at the same time, nor Mahler, nor Beethoven's late quartets. I enjoy listening to Chopin's piano music when I work. I'm not saying that Chopin's music is not as important, not at all, but it is a kind of music that somehow is right for that occasion. Western classical music has meant a lot to me and still does. It is something that I am still very far from knowing enough about. Really, to tell you frankly, I am still a pretty empty vessel.

VON BOEHM: *What does music have in common with architecture? I think it is the form, the structure, but also more.*

PEI: Architecture and music are both constructions of the mind. They need structure to give them form, which becomes the physical evidence of an idea. Then there is the element of time, which demands sequential experience within the construct which is space. Music and architecture both engage the senses with form, structure, color, and space.

VON BOEHM: *You know how to organize a building for an audience to be able to listen to a good Beethoven concert perfectly. You have proven it in Meyerson Symphony Hall. How did you do your studies for this wonderful symphony hall? I always have a feeling when I am there of being in a private house. For me it is an invitation to hear the music in a perfect, but very private way.*

PEI: I wish I could feel the same way about that project, the first and only project for a concert hall that I have ever done. When I was interviewed for that commission, I was already in my seventies. I mentioned to the committee that I loved music, but I knew very little about music. I wanted them to know that I love music. I wanted to do a symphony hall, and I did it . . . I like to think that I really should do a second one, because that hall is not the best that I could do; I know I could do a better hall now. I learned a lot from that one hall, but I also did something interesting. The reason why that hall turned out relatively successful was because I learned a great deal from my many visits to some of the great concert halls here and particularly in Europe, where classical music is rooted. I cannot imagine doing a symphony hall without having heard concerts at the Musikverein in Vienna or the Concertgebouw in Amsterdam. The emotional part of music has something to do with the cultural tradition of that country, of that place, and of that time. For me it is a new world and it will remain so. The scientific part of music is much easier for me, the physics of music. When it comes to acoustics, I can learn that. Not that I am a good acoustician, but I understand it. Western music affects me more than Eastern music, even though my mother was a musician. Somehow it doesn't have the same kind of richness that I find in Western music. Many of my Chinese friends disagree with me and say: "You don't know enough about Chinese music to make that comparison." Perhaps so. But emotionally I was completely overwhelmed when I first heard Beethoven. I still remain overwhelmed.

von Boehm: *I know that it was always one of your dreams to create a symphony hall in Beijing. Would it look different from a hall in Dallas, New York or Berlin?*

PEI: Yes. And, you know, indeed Beijing will build one. It is difficult. The symphony hall in China has to serve many purposes, not only music. That weakens it. You see what I mean? It cannot have Western music all the time, so how can you do a hall that is adaptable to many things? I was told that this time they would like to do a pure concert hall. So I hope they will. They have already had plans for a competition.

von Boehm: *Would a concert hall for Asian music . . . Chinese music . . . follow a completely different concept?*

PEI: Absolutely. First of all, symphony orchestras of the Western type simply did not exist in China. They are beginning to experiment with them. For me, Chinese music is best presented with very few instruments. A few instruments cannot be successful in a big hall: there is not enough volume. How can you design a symphony hall for both Chinese music and Western orchestras? It is very difficult. I'll tell you what I would like to do: I'd like to do a Chinese opera house. Chinese opera is very different from Western opera. It is a musical form that I have been brought up with and understand. It doesn't require elaborate machinery like that required by Western opera houses. It doesn't have any of that, it is very simple. I like that kind of opera, the "Kunqu" form in particular.

von Boehm: *It is more the people acting than the scene itself.*

PEI: Exactly—the facial expressions and the movements of hands and feet are of paramount importance. I don't think Chinese opera is suitable for three thousand people. Chinese opera is more like Japanese theater, something between Kabuki and Noh.

von Boehm: *Coming back to Western music, what did you want to express with your first symphony hall, the Meyerson Symphony Hall in Dallas? For me, it is music translated into architecture, with all the round shapes and circular forms we find there.*

PEI: That is the outside. That is the place where you go for intermission or when you arrive. The hall itself is very conservative. It is conservative for reasons I no longer accept. If I were to do another one today, I would not be so timid. I will tell you why. I feel that the hall doesn't fully represent what I would have liked to do. It was my first one.

I thought about it and finally was very much influenced by the successful halls of the West, which were all built in the eighteenth and nineteenth centuries. I also realized the music that they were likely to perform would have a good deal of Mozart, Schubert, Beethoven, and Brahms. Therefore the environment of the hall . . . I am talking about the hall itself and not the outside spaces . . . somehow had to be appropriate for that kind of music. I just didn't feel comfortable enough to create an entirely new twentieth-century environment for eighteenth- and nineteenth-century music. Do you see what I mean? I was diffident, and that diffidence shows. If I were to do it again, I would do it differently. I went to the Berlin Philharmonic to try to prove to myself that there is a new possibility. To begin with, the orchestra is more or less in the middle. It is a surround hall, which I actually think is OK. I could have accepted that. I was worried about the acoustics in that hall. They are not as good as at the Musikverein. I know if Herbert von Karajan were alive he would disagree with me. But that is how I felt. I felt that the Musikverein was a better hall for the projection of sound. I went to the concert hall in Amsterdam and I found it equally satisfying from an acoustic point of view.

VON BOEHM: *The circular shapes that you tried in Dallas, are they actually a tribute to music? I see it partially as a tribute to music, but also as a tribute to Baroque forms.*

PEI: Now you are talking about the enclosure. The building itself is a rectangular shoebox that was mandated by the symphony hall director, by the trustees and by the acoustician. When I entered the scene to accept the commission the acoustician was already selected. They had already agreed that the best halls in the world are the prototypes like Vienna and Boston, which is like a double-cube shoebox. That was a given, and had I come in earlier, I might have questioned that, but I had to accept it. Then the question was, what I have to work with besides surrounding the hall and the interior. I have already explained the inside. I was very, very conservative. I wanted to be more eighteenth and nineteenth century in spirit because of the music being played there. As for the outside of the hall, I felt the need to be free. Therefore, to wrap another form around the shoebox, I started to use curvilinear forms . . . as you said, Baroque. It does have some spatial excitement in that space for that reason.

VON BOEHM: *You do not draw a lot. You are not someone who draws every little bit of a project. It is just the concept that you draw—sometimes only roughly.*

PEI: When I first started my practice, I did draw a lot. Very quickly afterwards I found that I could draw faster in my head than I could draw on paper. The Beaux-Arts tradition with which I started my architectural training was based on drawings. Many wonderful ideas came out of making drawings, but I find that process too slow. For that reason I abandoned the idea, though not entirely. I still draw . . . I draw to express my ideas to the people who work with me. Those are sketched ideas and not drawings to please myself. They are not drawings to be framed.

VON BOEHM: *It gives you the freedom to leave things open to the end—you like that. And then you're able to correct things up until the very end, and you like that freedom.*

PEI: Also the freedom to eliminate. You can develop things in your mind very much more effectively. Then, to learn to be independent of drawings, one has to sharpen one's mind; because of social training, that is before computers, it is not so easy to say "I don't need to draw, I can draw in my mind and I can pretty much see what the building will be like." That is a training in itself. It wasn't that easy. I was not trained that way. By force of circumstance I have come to that practice. . . . I find it rather effective to do it that way. I can work at night without lights by drawing in my mind. Then I will check it in the morning. I have frequently found that I can construct a space in my mind. The computer today can do much the same thing that the mind can do. What I am doing now, which is constructing space in my mind, I have nothing to show for. I cannot record it; there is no printer. My brain can try different ideas, but there is nothing to print with. In the morning I don't have any evidence of what I've done. With a computer not only can you think quickly, but you also can print it. That is a great advance, I think.

VON BOEHM: *In your mind, in your imagination, you can always construct three-dimensional things. You can walk through spaces in your mind; the computer can do something similar but with a lot more effort, of course.*

PEI: I cannot carry a computer with me while I am listening to music or, for that matter, go to bed with it—which is where I do most of my thinking.

I.M. Pei as a student at Harvard University

The United States

VON BOEHM: *Do you remember the very moment of saying goodbye to China? On the President Coolidge—you left on that ship. Your relatives all came to say goodbye. Which images do you still keep in mind of that moment?*

PEI: I would have thought, looking back, that that would have been a rather emotional moment, which required sort of being very sad, maybe tears coming to my eyes when saying goodbye to my family and all that . . . but there was none of that. Not because I was hard-hearted but because the anticipation was so strong. The anticipation of seeing a new world had overcome all the other feelings of sadness. I had nothing but great expectations. I was not sad, though in fact my family was very sad to see me leave. I myself was not sad, I was rather expectant of a fantastic kind of adventure. I was alone. I was not even eighteen years old. I left my family for the first time. That was it. It was a very interesting moment. I expected myself to be very emotional, in tears, but not at all. I did not have any of that. I just thought about how lucky I was to have the opportunity to see a new world.

VON BOEHM: *So it came quite naturally to you to leave and explore further into a new space.*

PEI: Oh yes—I had dreamt about it a lot. I was so intensely hoping that this was going to happen. So that moment of separation from family and friends was not a sad one for me.

VON BOEHM: *What had you heard at the time about the United States? Why did you want to go there? What were the sources from which you were getting information about the U.S. in Shanghai?*

PEI: I had not seen the world except my own world, which was the east coast of China. Movies were for me more than entertainment, they were also important sources of information and imagination.

I almost never missed a film by Buster Keaton, Harold Lloyd, Charlie Chaplin, or Bing Crosby. Crosby's films in particular had a tremendous influence on my choosing the

United States instead of England to pursue my education. College life in the U.S. seemed to me to be mostly fun and games. Since I was too young to be serious, I wanted to be part of it.

VON BOEHM: *The cultural effect on people like yourself in Asia at that time was not to be underestimated. American movies were a powerful cultural force—as they are today, worldwide. Maybe because of, as you say, the lightness of it . . . because in Asia you don't feel a sense of lightness necessarily when you look at life.*

PEI: That is exactly right. It is different. Take something quite simple, for instance what we call college life. You could get a feeling for it in Bing Crosby's movies. College life in America seemed very exciting to me. It's not real, we know that. Nevertheless, at that time it was very attractive to me. I decided that was the country for me.

VON BOEHM: *Had you also been attracted to the aesthetic side of the skyscrapers you saw in those movies? There are famous film scenes that show the actors—like Harold Lloyd or Buster Keaton—hanging from the roof of a skyscraper or from a huge clock.*

PEI: Not so much . . . I was not so conscious of the architecture, but more about the lifestyle in America. The youth and freshness was one thing that came across, even then in the thirties. Whereas in China young people normally were very reluctant to express themselves. In China people were more inclined to be restrained. The States seemed to have a more easy-going lifestyle that was very appealing to me.

Remember, China is an old country. You respect tradition. People who are older than you—your uncle, your father—they are to be listened to. The feeling of having authority all around you . . . somehow you needed a release, and that release came from the movies.

VON BOEHM: *What did you miss most when you first came? I can very well imagine what you were looking for and what you finally found. You probably were very confirmed in your feeling that you had to leave and that you had to have this kind of life. But did you miss anything? What did you miss most?*

PEI: You miss the family. The excitement of the new can last quite a while, but before long you ask yourself: "What about my sisters, my brothers and my father?" I hadn't seen them for a long time . . . I had written them letters. Of course there was always this feeling of responsibility, the

Chinese sense of family is deep in me. What really made it bearable there for me was my work. It distracted me from sadness and worries. I had a lot of work. Like most foreign students I had a language problem. I had to work hard to catch up with my studies. So I didn't have too much time to think about home.

VON BOEHM: *Work is always a good cure.*

PEI: It is always a good cure; when you have not enough to occupy you, then sadness sets in. Also, there was a community of foreign students at the university, many of whom were from the Orient. That helped me somehow to make up for the loss.

VON BOEHM: *Did you come with the intention to stay? Probably you just wanted to come for four or five years.*

PEI: I came to study, to learn, so that I could return and serve the country. For the Chinese of my generation, patriotism was a very powerful force. I wanted China to become prosperous and strong. I wanted to contribute.

VON BOEHM: *Then something must have happened which prevented you from going back. When was that point in time, and what was your motivation?*

PEI: The war. What instilled that sense of patriotism in me was the conflict with Japan, the Japanese conquest of China, in 1931, Manchuria, in 1937, Shanghai. I did not forget those years. After MIT and Harvard, I was ready to go home, but the country was at war, civil war. I was ready to return, but my father told me to stay. That was the best advice I had ever received. I am deeply grateful to him for that.

VON BOEHM: *So you stayed. And you stayed for fifty years. You have been cut off for more than fifty years from the culture you came from. What helped you to still keep it in your inner self so strongly? I mean, you still have it in you.*

PEI: It really was a long stretch. I left China in 1935 and I did not have an opportunity to return until 1974. There was as always a community here in the United States that filled in that gap, not really well, but . . . there were a lot of young Chinese who were in the same situation that I was in. By then of course I had also made many American friends. Therefore that made up for the loss. I was very fortunate to meet Eileen, who later became my wife, and who studi-ed landscape design at Harvard after graduation from Wellesley. She was caught here for the same reason. Together, in our first home we created a little garden—very small but very Chinese. With some grasses and flowers which reminded us of China. My love for gardening probably has its roots in that time. I have a place in the country where I tried my hand at working with nature. I think I'm not very popular with the environmentalists in my community because I frequently cut down trees. The reason is that I want the good trees to survive and flourish. Nature and man working together, that is in my blood and I brought it from China. That is why working with nature helped me to overcome the loss of my country to a certain extent. But yes, I still find that separation rather wrenching. If I had gone back, probably I would be a very different person than I am today. I don't know what kind of person, but very different.

VON BOEHM: *When did you first learn about the architects who later became your masters and were very influential on you?*

PEI: In the beginning, in my early years, I was very much influenced by Le Corbusier, and by his three published volumes, which I found by coincidence at the library. Or maybe it wasn't coincidence, because I was actually quite unhappy with the state of my education, and I was looking for inspiration. Le Corbusier's three books were my bible. They were the only thing I could rely on to see anything new in architecture. I cannot forget Le Corbusier's visit to MIT in November 1935, dressed in black, with his thick glasses. The two days with Le Corbusier, or "Corbu" as we used to call him, were probably the most important days in my architectural education.

VON BOEHM: *You must have been interested as well in the work of Frank Lloyd Wright, who didn't like Le Corbusier at all. He called him "a painter and pamphleteer."*

PEI: I certainly was interested in his work. I even went to Spring Green, Wisconsin, to take a look at his Taliesin East building. I will never forget that day. When I got there in my old Chevy I drove into the estate and found myself surrounded by huge dogs. They barked and pounded on my car—I drove away. That was my loss, I suppose. I have always admired Wright's work, but Corbu was my early influence.

VON BOEHM: —*whom you met at Harvard's architecture school, where you went after MIT. The Bauhaus had been among the first institutions the Nazi regime had closed, and*

Walter Gropius and his family had fled to England and then to the United States, where he was offered the directorship of the Harvard Graduate School of Design.

PEI: . . . where he really felt free to express himself, the avant-garde ideas which he had developed as the founder of Bauhaus. I met him, and I said, "Of course!" Gropius was the actual reason for me to go to Harvard. Europe in those days was much ahead of us in the field of architecture. Harvard had acknowledged that. Gropius brought with him to Harvard a methodology of teaching that integrated architecture with all its related disciplines, as he had done in Bauhaus. He brought with him Martin Wagner to teach urban planning, László Moholy-Nagy on graphic design, and Marcel Breuer on architecture. What was missing were painters like Oskar Schlemmer and Paul Klee, who were so influential at Bauhaus. Like many young architects of my time, I was attracted to the school in a move that proved to be pivotal in my development as an architect.

VON BOEHM: *How would you describe the atmosphere at the school?*

PEI: Very exciting times indeed! The idea of Bauhaus at Harvard attracted some of the best students from everywhere. This magnetic effect made the Harvard Graduate School of Design a very exciting place. Gropius and also Breuer were the magnets and they should get credit for its success.

VON BOEHM: *What did you learn from Marcel Breuer for instance? Can you describe that?*

PEI: He was my best friend and teacher at Harvard. My wife and I traveled with him and his wife Connie to Greece twice. We were on a boat for three weeks each time—when you stay with someone for three weeks on a boat, you get to know him very well. He was a very warm person. While on board we rarely talked about architecture. He was very much interested in light, light which brings in shadows. He kept talking about light and shadow. If there is anything special in Greece, it is that special quality of light. So I became much more aware, let's say through his way of looking at light, of the importance of light on architecture.

VON BOEHM: *How do you like to use light in your buildings?*

PEI: Very important. I have to say since those early years with Breuer, I have become sensitized to the importance of light. Of course, I came to look at it not with his eyes, but with my own eyes. Light continued to play a very important role in my work. Early Cubist sculpture, which I am very fond of, would be impossible to appreciate without light. As a matter of fact, almost any sculpture is impossible to appreciate without light. Therefore you can extend that to architecture. I would say that light for me is of paramount importance to buildings. Without the play of light, form is inert and space becomes static; I would like to think that when I design buildings light is one of my first considerations.

VON BOEHM: *What about the importance of movement? You have to motivate people to move in buildings. How can you do that?*

PEI: You have to make it exciting. You know, that is something I learned from the Chinese gardens. Chinese gardens are always built in a very small place because there are so many people and the land is so limited. Within a very small piece of land, one can create maximum variety. Why? Because of the constantly changing perspective. It is the opposite of gardens like Versailles. The Oriental garden is designed to engage the visitor with a series of surprises. Once you think you have seen the most exciting object, a rock or something, and then you turn around and see something else. And then you turn again—constant movement and change. In designing space you also have to do that. You have to create surprises so that you make people want to discover more. You make people turn left, turn right or go straight ahead. So you do have to motivate—that is the word you have to use—people to look and explore.

VON BOEHM: *That is exactly what nature does. Nature is always in motion. If you look at tiny little structures like bacteria, which are invisible without a microscope, there is constant movement, constant surprise.*

PEI: Yes, I am very much aware of that. Those things came to me as time went on. If I use light in my buildings it is using the forces of nature. If I use geometric structures to give some rigidity to, let's say, a huge high-rise building like the Bank of China in Hong Kong, I am recognizing the forces of nature. It seems so natural, so fundamental, and yet to be sensitized to it takes time.

VON BOEHM: *Breuer made you aware of how important light is and at the same time made you look at life as a whole picture. What did you learn from Walter Gropius?*

PEI: From him I learned about discipline and the application of discipline.

VON BOEHM: *So what kind of a person was Walter Gropius?*

PEI: Most people think of Walter Gropius as someone strict, a disciplinarian. I learned discipline from him, but he was not the strict disciplinarian people think of and associate with him. He was a very warm person. My wife and I lived in his house for a summer in Lincoln. We got to know each other quite well. He did insist on reasoning, that you have to have a reason for doing certain things. You don't just do certain things because you enjoy doing them or because you like to or because it is interesting; you have to have a reason for it. Breuer was different. Breuer was more likely to let the emotional side be a factor in one's reasoning process. Whereas Gropius was a very rational individual. He was not at all rigid in the sense of his method of teaching. You see, to me he was a great teacher. As an architect, that is another subject of discussion. As a teacher he was one of the best because he allowed each of us to think for ourselves. We had to defend, we had to rationalize; we had to explain why we did certain things. At the same time, he was open. He loved to talk about the importance of relationships between technology and architecture, and mechanization, which he felt would discipline the world. Therefore we created certain forms which became our environment. He was passionate in his belief. I came from another world. I was a little less disciplined and less rational. So, from time to time I offered an alternative opinion. What about the relationship between history and architecture; between culture and architecture; climate and architecture? They all have an influence that would affect the strict relationship between technique and art . . . "Well, maybe you have a point," he would say. That is important. If he had said no, that there is no alternative to his principles, then I would have been crushed. He said, "Yes, explore it. Prove it to me," and that sort of thing. So I owe him a great deal for that reason, because he opened a student up and allowed him to explore on his own. You had to defend yourself; but you had to have a reason for it, not just because emotionally you thought this was a wonderful thing or a beautiful thing. That discipline was very useful.

VON BOEHM: *Maybe it was very important to have these two influences and create a symbiosis out of it. Breuer here and Gropius there. Maybe that is part of your secret, even, and part of the success of your architecture.*

PEI: That is precisely why I owe so much to those years at Harvard. The symbiosis between Breuer and Gropius created a very exciting environment for young architects. And I certainly don't regret the time at MIT. There I learned the science and technique of building, which is just as essential to architecture.

VON BOEHM: *Someone who told you that you should put your engineering studies aside was William Emerson, who was dean at MIT at the time when you were there. What was your relationship with him?*

PEI: William Emerson was a descendant of Ralph Waldo Emerson. He was a typical cultivated Bostonian. He would have been more at home at Harvard than at MIT. It was my good fortune that he took a liking to me. He represented that side of American history and culture that I was anxious to know about, and hence he became an important influence in my early years in America. He was indeed the one who persuaded me to become an architect. MIT is the oldest architectural school in the United States, a fact that is not generally known. And in the school of architecture, it has a department of architectural engineering. So it was very easy to drift into the engineering side of architecture. I thought for a time that I was more likely to succeed in that area, as an engineer, rather than as an architect. It was Emerson to whom I confided my lack of confidence in myself as an architect. He told me, "Young man, that is rubbish. I have never yet met a Chinese who cannot draw." He was generalizing. Of course it is not true, but it was his way of saying, "Don't be discouraged, stay and study architecture." Otherwise I could very well have become an engineer. I decided that was a turning point. I said, "Alright, if you think so, then I will continue."

VON BOEHM: *What was the subject of your architectural thesis at MIT?*

PEI: That was 1939. As I mentioned earlier I had a duty to the country, I guess because of the sad state of affairs in China at that time, the many indignities that the country had suffered. That feeling was deeply ingrained in me. When I decided to find a subject for my thesis, I was thinking about how to contribute something to China. It is a large country, where in the 1930s, 85 percent of the population could not read or write. There were no newspapers outside of the big cities. I proposed several types of prototypical prefabricated units built of bamboo where news and entertainment could be obtained, to be placed in remote villages and communities. Broadcasting centers would be located in nearby cities, as radio had already been in common use. So this was the subject I chose for my thesis, and I called it "propaganda units for China." Oh, what a title! My professor could not accept it because propaganda was a bad word in those years. In the 1930s, Goebbels had made propaganda a bad word in America. I don't know why I used that word. The professor said he would accept my program but not my title. I used it in spite of the objection because to me that is what it was. It was a kind of public education. I couldn't think of a stronger word than propaganda. Of course, looking back at it now, my professor was right. There was a better word for it, "information." I rather wish I had records of that thesis.

VON BOEHM: *What you had in mind were mobile units?*

PEI: Yes, and they could be added to and expanded. They could actually build it . . . I also used color. I remember the bamboo panels were woven and they were colored with primary colors: black, red, green and blue. By moving these panels we could announce to the villages what was going on. I wrote all those things out . . . but anyway that was my thesis. I didn't really have good guidance. Those were the years when American architectural education was still at an uncertain stage. That was the time when Gropius came to Harvard. I told Dean Emerson, "After I finish school here I would like to go to Harvard." He was furious. I have never seen him so angry. His face was completely red. He must have been seventy-seven years old at that time, and I was so afraid that he would have a heart attack! I was one of his favorite students, and I was abandoning what he believed in and going to someone like Gropius, whom he despised. It was almost like I was going to the enemy camp.

VON BOEHM: *Which you did in fact. And in the "enemy camp" the so-called dead knowledge of art history had already been expunged by Gropius. Goodbye, Gothic and Renaissance.*

PEI: I wanted to break away. Gropius represented to me an opportunity to see the new. Which didn't mean that I agreed with him always and on every point.

VON BOEHM: *What did you think about his theory of the mechanization of the world, which he had already developed by the time?*

PEI: I think it was more the context of that theory than the theory itself… The difference between Gropius' ideas and mine were, if I may use the word "difference," really in the term "international style." Anyway, that was the big subject then. Gropius believed firmly that because the world is being industrialized at different paces—the West first then the East later—sooner or later the whole world will be industrialized. It means that the words "international style," which Le Corbusier also used, will eventually sweep the world. I was not so sure at that time. It seemed too rigid to me. I thought, there must be more to architecture. But I couldn't yet define what it was. I was still too young.

VON BOEHM: *In 1943 World War II was still going on, and you went to serve in the NDRC, the National Defense Research Committee in Princeton, New Jersey, for two and a half years. What could an architect do there?*

PEI: They told me: "If you know how to build you should also know how to destroy." In fact one of my first projects was how to bomb Germany. They wanted me to study the structure of bridges, for instance, and then wanted me to develop measures to destroy them. But before I even had any notion about the best way to bomb Germany, the war with Germany was already over. Then they said I had to learn how to bomb Japan. That was a different subject because Japanese buildings at the time were mostly constructed of wood and paper. The high explosives being used in Europe would not be very efficient—I was asked to develop a kind of incendiary bomb instead. This was a very sad part of my life. I don't want to talk about it. I came back after the war—probably more mature then in a way—and re-entered Harvard. Then Gropius said, "Now, you were good before . . . but now you are back, I want you to feel free to express yourself and what you want to do." Eventually he said I should stay and teach. I did not have a degree yet at that time, so it was a very high compliment. It was at that moment that I said I would like to prove something to myself, that there is a limit to the internationalization of architecture. The reason why I said that was because there are differences in the world such as climate, history, culture and life. All these things must play a part in the architectural expression. The peoples of the world are so different. Gropius said, "Well you know my views. But if you think you're right, go ahead and prove it. It would be very interesting." So I chose a subject, which was to design a museum for Shanghai. What could I possibly take as a model? Greek or Roman? But somehow I could not imagine Chinese artifacts in that kind of a place, or even Chinese paintings in that kind of a building. I said that I was going to select that as my subject. I made my design—it was quite Cubist in a way—and presented it to the faculty. Marcel Breuer thought it was the most important project that Harvard had ever produced. He told the student body that. It had been a great challenge and now I was quite happy about it. Breuer and Gropius were not alike. Breuer in many ways was much less orthodox, much more free to accept propositions such as the one I tried to prove. He found that proof in my project. It was very important for Harvard to know and for the student to understand that there are cultural differences that should be expressed in architecture.

VON BOEHM: *What was the main concept in this project? You wanted to create a space in which objects such as jades, pots and vessels could be displayed. What was the spirit of it?*

PEI: It was really a container for art objects that are very different from Western art objects. European art, from the Renaissance to the nineteenth century, was mostly commissioned to celebrate the power of the church and the state. The art of the Orient, by which I mean China, Korea, and Japan, on the other hand, was created largely for private enjoyment. Important paintings, for example, were not hung on a wall for long periods of time. Rather, they were unrolled, looked at and enjoyed, and rolled back up again. Not long ago, my wife and I made a special request through the Ministry of Culture of Japan to view an important Zen painting by the painter Muchi at a temple in Kyoto. Fortunately for us, it was a dry sunny autumn day, and we were allowed to examine it for an hour. The priest in charge told us in all solemnity that he would not unroll the painting even for the Emperor if the weather were harmful to the painting. These differences in life and culture must have their effects on the design of museums to conserve and exhibit art.

VON BOEHM: *You designed very simple structures for the building, but you also designed little gardens and courtyards around it.*

PEI: Yes, a scholar's study or retreat invariably has a small garden attached to it. It is here that paintings and calligraphy are made and enjoyed. Art and gardens are inseparable.

VON BOEHM: *The museum that you designed at Harvard had many courtyards, and now it has many offspring. I have the same feeling in the National Gallery, for example. It is kind of small in scale. I don't have the feeling that I am in a huge museum. I have the same impression in the Miho Museum you designed in Japan—that I am in a private house. I can concentrate on the objects and am actually not distracted by the architecture. On the contrary: the architecture supports my concentration—and that is quite rare.*

PEI: Finally I had an opportunity to do this in real buildings at the Fragrant Hill Hotel close to Beijing. For me it is a rather serious piece of work as someone who had left China for a long time and returned. I might not have noticed the many changes that took place during my absence, but looking back at it, I think the design is still valid. Chinese life has not changed. Those Chinese who have visited the place and have stayed there continue to come back and say they feel really at home in it. The reason why I don't go back is because they have made such a mess of it. The design is not revolutionary. It is not something they have never seen before. It is something all too familiar to them. It has become a prototype for many small garden hotels in China. I am pleased with that.

VON BOEHM: *That is the tension between the new and the familiar, which is always wonderful and creative—and also for the spectator. He himself becomes a part of the creative process. Marcel Duchamp has written about that. You can be stunned by something completely new, and yet you discover something familiar in it. Not to cross this line completely, so that there is still a little bit of the familiar, is great—and this is true for the other arts as well, for example, in certain forms of abstraction.*

PEI: I agree with that. And the special thing about architecture is that it is closely related to life. Look at Frank Lloyd Wright's work. He is celebrated as the most important architect of the twentieth century in the United States, but there is nothing unusual about his work. These little things make all the difference, not revolutionary changes. Architecture particularly is a continuum; it follows life and life does not change very abruptly. Then there were times in history when abrupt change was unavoidable and necessary.

In my opinion, Cubism is really the genesis of modern architecture. Some people ask, "Where does modern architecture begin?" In 1850? . . . No, not really. The industrial revolution? . . . Yes, maybe, because we used steel. The Crystal Palace in England . . . middle of the nineteenth century? Is that the time? Maybe, maybe not. But then when Cubism came it was much clearer: it was a real turning point for architecture, which was strongly influenced by that art. It began with Cézanne. Then came Picasso, who worked together with Braque. After the first ten years of Cubism, Braque no longer participated and Picasso went on. He developed Cubism in many forms . . . pictorially. Some of his drawings and paper constructions were completely Cubistic. Their influence on architecture is unbelievable.

VON BOEHM: *Maybe that is because he showed that, through Cubism, we can understand physical movements and feelings in a completely new way. Cubism can open the eyes to everything that is physical. And good architecture, for me, always provokes physical feelings, because the body finds itself in a different context.*

PEI: Absolutely right. Some people call it a "stage" for the body but it goes much deeper than that—this is exactly what you are talking about. It is about the solid and the void. What else is there in architecture when you talk about form and space? It is the play between the solids and the voids. Therefore, the effect of light on those solids and voids is so important. And there you cannot separate architecture from painting or sculpture. It was never more graphically evident than in Picasso's work.

As I wanted to learn more about Picasso and Cubism, I sought out Jacques Lipchitz, who was then living in Hastings, New York. We became good friends in the fifties and sixties. I admired his early work, which showed strong affinities to Cubism. In retrospect, I admit that some of my work was influenced by Cubism, such as the National Center for Atmospheric Research (1956), the Everson Museum (1964), and the East Wing of the National Gallery of Art (1978).

VON BOEHM: *Do you see another break coming in the near future?*

Drawing of the Everson Museum of Art, Syracuse, New York

PEI: Yes, something very interesting is happening in which I am no longer a participant. It is the computer. Frank Gehry's work, for instance, is not possible without a computer. Nobody can draw it. Will that lead us to a new architecture? Cubism did. There is no question about it. If the computer will have a similar powerful effect—time will tell.

VON BOEHM: *I think Frank Gehry's work and the work that the computer has permitted still stands on the shoulders of Cubism.*

PEI: Of course it is standing on the shoulders of Cubism. Because it has a certain structure. This is where I come back to the city; the city is rather rigidly geometric. You never can separate a building from the place where it's standing. Gehry's museum in Bilbao is just right at that place. If you would move it into the city, it would be impossible. Also because of the materials. You can not do that kind of building with stone. Therefore permanence is also an issue. You cannot do it with stone because of the complex shape. You have to use sheets of metal like shingles. The result can be stunning, as in Bilbao.

VON BOEHM: *Maybe architecture today is not about permanence any longer because our age is not about permanence.*

PEI: That is right. The other day I saw a video recording about Peter Eisenman, who won the competition for a School of Architecture building in Cincinnati, Ohio. One of the participants in the symposium said that it will fall down in two years. The sense of permanence . . . I'm old fashioned enough to still believe in it. I am open enough to feel that a change will come. Now the new technology has made it possible to make incredible drawings. Have you ever seen the plans of Bilbao? They are incredibly beautiful. You cannot draw that by hand—it has to be done with software. It is like building an airplane. I look at it with a certain amount of envy, and I wish I were younger. I have always believed that art leads the way for architecture. Now it is technology's turn. But art will always be there to inspire architecture.

VON BOEHM: *Maybe the architecture we were just talking about which is today's contemporary architecture is also following art in a way. In art today you don't have much permanence anymore. You don't have that constraint. You don't have breakthroughs and you don't have permanence. It is just quoting things that have been around this century—I think it's because we have had so many great artists and artistic breakthroughs in the twentieth century. Therefore, what we see now in the best case is a kind of borrowed permanence. For three years you have this artist who is promoted and then you have another one.*

PEI: But the lack of permanence can be very important in the sense that you can experiment in art. To experiment in architecture could be costly. It is really difficult. If you do it on a canvas it is not the same. You cannot just say, "spend a million dollars to build an experiment." No client would accept that. Therefore, we need the other arts to break the wave for us. But we must not be seduced into thinking that experimenting in painting and sculpture is going to be applicable to architecture.

I.M. Pei at the Webb & Knapp office, ca. 1958

New York City and Beyond

VON BOEHM: *Let's talk a little about your time in New York City when you first went there. There was the need or the urge, I suppose, to apply what you had learned at MIT and Harvard with Breuer and Gropius. And then, in New York City, you entered a completely different universe—the world of William Zeckendorf.*

PEI: William Zeckendorf was perhaps one of the most imaginative land developers, if not the most imaginative. When he sent for me to come to work for him, I accepted simply because I wanted to learn something about real estate. But to my surprise I learned a lot more from this man. Since I had come to the U.S., I had very rarely moved outside of the academic environment. He was the one who introduced me to an entirely new world. So I owe a great deal to him. Because he was so imaginative he wanted to try so many new things, new ideas. Of course, many of those ideas never got built. I did a lot of design, but I constructed very little in those ten years. However, the knowledge I gained from working for him served me well afterwards.

VON BOEHM: *What was the most important thing you learned from him personally? Because now your two worlds really clashed together, in a way. He was completely westernized, a developer who never left the country. He came from a very different world. What could you take from his world?*

PEI: You usually learn the most from someone who is just the opposite of you. If I were to think of someone who is my exact opposite, I would say it was William Zeckendorf, and because of that we became great friends. His son, Bill Jr., was here the other night for dinner, and to me he was like my brother. You know, that relationship developed all in ten years' time. I learned a lot about the politics of building.

There was a very important government program called "Title One" of the Federal Housing Act of 1949, which encouraged slum clearance in U.S. cities. It was initiated under Eisenhower, and in order to participate in urban development, one had to get involved with the cities' mayors, and governors . . . and Zeckendorf knew them all. Through him I was introduced into the world of politics, which served me well. I don't think I had ever met a mayor until I came to New York. Since then and those ten years, I don't know how many governors and mayors I have met. We went from city to city in his private DC-3. That was a very important experience for a young man like myself. Also, on the human side, I learned something else from him. I learned the importance of being generous. He was a very generous man. Generosity is a virtue in life. I learned that from him.

VON BOEHM: *I think you take great pleasure in the game side of architecture, with politics and everything else.*

PEI: I don't know if I would call it a game because it is not an easy kind of game to play. But it is a challenge. I would not have been able to survive in Paris—now that you have mentioned it I come to think about it—were it not for the fact that I had already encountered that kind of problem when I was with Zeckendorf. It is not very easy to sell an idea to a city or a state, to demolish a large area in the center of the city and build something new. It called for a tremendous amount of patience and understanding of the world of politics. I learned that, and that helped me develop patience and understanding of how a society works, the power structure behind any major civic undertaking. That was something that I must say that I learned from Zeckendorf. And also I learned that good ideas are worth nothing without good allies who support them. First, from 1948 to 1960, twelve years, I worked exclusively for Zeckendorf. He was a man with tremendous energy and imagination. He wanted to express those ideas architecturally. I happened to be the person he was looking for. I organized a team to work under me and try out his ideas in urban development. In 1946 he was already famous for bringing the United Nations to New York. His development proposals were front-page news in New York, Washington, Denver, or Montreal. The 1949 National Housing Act became his vehicle.

VON BOEHM: *And "Title One" of that act was of most special importance for you.*

PEI: It was important for me, and especially important for Zeckendorf. Until then he had always had to borrow money in order to implement his ambitious proposals. He said, "Now I don't have to go to the bankers . . . I have Uncle Sam." American cities in those days were not in very good shape; slums were prevalent in or near the center of cities. Zeckendorf's idea was to take advantage of the need to rid the cities of these slums and thus provide incentive to rebuild. The federal, state, and city governments jointly underwrote the costs of acquiring the land. In other words, once a piece of land was designated as substandard, prospective developers like Zeckendorf would propose a plan for redevelopment. If the proposal were accepted—and they had to go through many bureaucratic steps—the government would then underwrite the land value. That is tremendous, because you can start with almost no investment in the land.

VON BOEHM: *But you have the profit at the end because you have the building.*

PEI: That is exactly how it worked. You have to build your plan, and if you do it right, then you profit from it. Zeckendorf often said to me, "Now I have Uncle Sam as my banker." We went to all the big cities of the United States, and I helped him identify areas that needed development. We flew in his private airplane to visit cities that provided opportunities for redevelopment. It gave me an opportunity to meet governors, mayors, development officials, and the prominent citizens of many communities. It also gave me the opportunity to understand the nature of the city as an organism, so that I could propose the kind of development that was needed. It was a wonderful training ground for me, in spite of the limitations—architecturally speaking—as those projects involved mostly low-cost housing.

VON BOEHM: *What could you, as an architect, do within the framework of a project like that? What was your concept? What was your goal? To give good housing to the people is one goal. Aesthetically, you have to consider the cityscape.*

PEI: What was important was creating livable housing at the lowest possible cost, with the highest possible architectural and planning standards. That was clearly a challenge, and my associates and I can recall with satisfaction some small accomplishments in this area.

VON BOEHM: *Where for instance?*

PEI: I would look today with great pride at Philadelphia. The district of Society Hill was a slum. All around prostitutes were walking the streets. Today it is probably one of the more prestigious neighborhoods. Not every project has that kind of success story. But there are two others in New

York: one is the Kips Bay apartments, and the other is three high-rise apartment towers for New York University, south of Washington Square.

VON BOEHM: *You did Courthouse Square in Denver also.*

PEI: Courthouse Square was something different. It was not exactly urban renewal. It was not housing, it was the conversion of a department store into a hotel; a new store, and a large parking garage. In other words, the federal, state, and city governments took over the property, wrote the cost down, and turned it over for development. The developer had to present them with a plan; once approved, it had to be executed. Mr. Zeckendorf told me that someday his company Webb & Knapp would become the General Motors of real estate. He had accumulated a lot of property without much investment. In order to realize a profit, he had to develop the property. In order to build he still had to go to the bankers, and he once again found himself indebted to them.

VON BOEHM: *Was it at that time that you really learned to think in the context of the city? That is what I find in your work later. I mean, you can do the Grand Louvre for instance in many different ways. For many architects it would have been enough for them to have this huge building, to create, to excavate and to build a new entrance hall—but to think about opening this whole space and the Cour Napoleon to connect the two sides of the River Seine is a different thing. This shows me that you still think of the urban context, all the time. In Washington it was the same.*

PEI: That's right. I learned the process of development and about the city as a living organism. That knowledge was invaluable to me for a project like the Louvre. The Louvre, as is generally recognized, is a city within a city. From the twelfth to the middle of the nineteenth century it was built by a succession of kings as an ever-expanding palace. For more than 800 meters along the River Seine it was a barrier between the two parts of Paris. When President Mitterrand decided in 1981 to transform it in its totality into Louvre-the-museum, the possibility of joining the two banks of the city became a byproduct of his decision. The wall which the Louvre once was could become the vibrant heart of Paris. In retrospect, designing Louvre-the-museum is a far cry from designing low-cost housing but the underlying challenge is the same.

VON BOEHM: *When you were still with Zeckendorf, that was when you started to think about how to make low-cost housing exciting—that is, affordable and still an exciting task for an architect.*

PEI: I learned a lot about that from Mies van der Rohe. This is the period when I started to look at Mies' buildings. I went to Chicago to see him. He had just designed two towers along North Michigan Avenue. I looked at it and said to myself: "How beautiful." I thought that was the way to go—architecturally. Then I thought about it again and I said: "Could we afford to build that?" No, it was too expensive. Why was it so expensive? Well, it was the curtain wall which was added on to the structure. This was the beginning of Kips Bay in Manhattan. Kips Bay was done with the structure as the facade. All we needed to do was to put in a piece of glass. Mies had the structure and then attached to it a glass and aluminum skin. That makes two or three dollars' per-square-foot difference, but it is just enough to have made it unfeasible to compete with low-cost housing projects at that time. Kips Bay is still there, and people love to live in it. Its success as urban housing is also because we proposed in our site plan a large private park within the development.

VON BOEHM: *But the way to this success was quite a rocky road, because actually you and Zeckendorf had to overcome many obstacles.*

PEI: Yes, the project almost died. Zeckendorf brought in Turner Construction and Fuller Construction to make estimates. Both came in at eighteen dollars a square foot. When these two estimates came in at the same price I suspected something, and Zeckendorf did, too. He then invited me to lunch and told me that we had to drop the project. I remember this conversation very well. He told me, "The maximum that I can spend is 10 percent more than the prevailing cost of this type of housing, and that is ten to eleven dollars per square foot. The estimates are almost double." "I am very sad," I said. He said, "I'm sad too. I still remember you told me something about building low-cost housing with brick. You told me then that a bricklayer used to lay 800 bricks a day. Today they lay only 500 bricks a day with a helper. I believed in you when you told me that. This approach for building low-cost housing is out for the near future. It appears that architectural concrete is not a viable alternative either." I said, "Well, you are right. I am sorry." At the end of our lunch he said, "Well, maybe we are ahead of our time," but he didn't give up so quickly. A few weeks later he came back to me and said, "Young man, I have someone I want you to meet. I am going to buy his company, an industrial engineering company that specializes in building concrete highways and bridges. I am going to buy that company because he said that he can build your building." That was Zeckendorf, he never gave up. To achieve what we both wanted he simply ignored the big construction companies and bought his own. They built the project and it came in at $10.15 per square foot. In the end it was not the cheapest—I was wrong—the cheapest was still to build in brick. Zeckendorf was important to me because of his spirit of adventure. He placed a high value on ideas. My satisfaction came from that relationship. Because of that I worked for him for a long time for little money. For almost ten years we replaced substandard sections of cities with low-cost housing of quality and sound planning. Looking back, I am quite proud of those projects.

VON BOEHM: *It was very good training. But didn't you have a feeling that it was a little bit too long? And it didn't bring a lot of prestige. I imagine that many of your colleagues who saw themselves as artists disapproved of the fact that you were working for Zeckendorf.*

PEI: You're probably right. But I didn't care much because I knew exactly how precious that kind of training was. Probably it was longer than I needed to. If I had left a few years earlier I would have learned all that I needed to learn. But then the opportunities would not have been there for me. Once you identify with one type of work it is very difficult to get into another kind of work. Even so, I was told that my name was on the long list to be considered for the design of parts of Lincoln Center. I never reached the final list, as I had no experience and therefore no credibility in the design of monumental public architecture.

VON BOEHM: *You could use the skills you learned with Zeckendorf in a very practical way for the first time in a very big project when Mrs. Jacqueline Kennedy came to you and asked you to build the Kennedy Library.*

PEI: That was more luck than anything else. I had built very little at that time, very little that I could show her. I think it was a question of sympathy, or chemistry, as people call it. I felt very comfortable with the lady and I think she felt very comfortable with me. I think that was the principal reason why she chose me. She had the best architects in the world to choose from. They were all extremely interested in the project because of the emotional response to the assassination of Jack Kennedy. I was certainly one of them.

VON BOEHM: *Was the Kennedy Library the project with the biggest constraints for you?*

PEI: In the Kennedy Library project, we encountered unexpected difficulties. The project lasted fourteen years (1965–79), and ten of those years were spent searching for a site. In the process, my associate Theodore Musho and I made dozens of schemes, each one for a different site. We were all emotionally and creatively exhausted. I could have done a lot better if I were able to do it fresh from the very beginning. That was a historic moment to do something important. As time went on it lost its force. I remember when I first went into a community to talk about the Kennedy Library, everybody was just so expectant of a wonderful project. In a few years the mood had changed because of the Vietnam war. That was a consequence of circumstances beyond our control.

VON BOEHM: *Still, there was and there is a philosophical concept behind this building. I feel it when I go there. The huge space that is empty, with just the American flag.*

PEI: That part of it is right, although it could have been done in a more exciting way. I think the best part of that is in the siting. The site was a dump surrounded by a public housing project. The water at low tide smells very bad. When I first looked at it my heart sank. The challenge for us was to remake the site and put the building at the very tip. That was right.

VON BOEHM: *It has a very beautiful view because you see Boston and the Hancock Tower in the sunset and the Harbor. It is like a painting where you see the structure through the windows.*

PEI: In that respect the siting was a success. That was a project full of challenges and problems but it did not come out the way I dreamed it would due to circumstances . . . beyond anybody's control.

VON BOEHM: *What remained was the wonderful friendship with Jacqueline Kennedy Onassis.*

PEI: Yes, that lasted until the end. We became friends and were quite close on a private basis. But she was no longer a client. She married Onassis in 1966 and she left the project afterwards. From that point on it was without leadership. I don't mean organizational leadership; I mean spiritual leadership. First Robert Kennedy died and then she left. Teddy Kennedy had a lot of other problems. The project became an orphan.

VON BOEHM: *Do you remember the very day when Mrs. Kennedy first came to your office to discuss the Kennedy Library project with you?*

PEI: How can I forget? . . . I could never forget that. We had nothing much to show to her. No big concert halls, museums or the like. My work had been unglamorous: slum clearance, low-cost housing. But she took a deep interest in that and constantly asked: "Why? Why? Why?" She wanted to know everything. We had repainted our small studio. In our tiny reception area we had put a beautiful bouquet of flowers. She immediately saw it and said: "What a beautiful bouquet—do you always have those flowers?" I told her honestly that we had just bought them for her. Then, I told her that it was much too early for me to say how the Kennedy Library would look. How could I have known at this point in time? I had to tell her honestly. Maybe that was exactly what convinced her.

In any case—that day was perhaps a turning point for me. In 1964, when Mrs. Kennedy first chose me, I thought that was the most important commission in my life. I really did and I still do, because it made me known to the American public and because of that it was easier for me to be accepted by other clients. But the fact that it didn't quite turn out the way I had hoped . . . was a disappointment to me. It should have been a great project.

VON BOEHM: *If you're summing up—what is really missing from this project?*

PEI: The inspiration was missing. I think there was a loss of energy and ambition in ourselves, architect and client. Deep in my heart I know that it could have been much better if circumstances were different. I wanted to give something very special to the memory of President Kennedy. It could and should have been a great project.

VON BOEHM: *Do you have a dream?*

PEI: No one can say one does not have a dream. But I am so busy trying to realize possible dreams, that I don't have time to think about lost dreams. Really, I am being frank about it. I'm engaged and I am happy with what has been offered to me. It is true that I was always very selective. I had to be, and even more so today, now that time becomes more and more limited for me. I consider myself very fortunate to have had the opportunity to realize some "dream" projects in my career. So why should I worry?

VON BOEHM: *What is the most wonderful moment in a "possible dream?" When you go into a building for the first time and it is finished, or is it the groundbreaking, or the process of creating a first idea after months of research? Which moment do you enjoy the most?*

PEI: What I enjoy the most is recalling the process of overcoming the difficulties, all the problems I had to face, and all the help I got from various people, especially from project collaborators and my clients—flashbacks of the history of the project. One likes to celebrate the satisfaction of accomplishment.

VON BOEHM: *Matisse once stated: "You should never, ever forget to see the world through a child's eyes." And there is also a very similar remark by Mencius, the Chinese philosopher. Do you think they are both right?*

PEI: I think so. A child's eye is open and innocent, uncluttered with the debris of life, which enables him to get to the essence of things. On the other hand, wisdom comes from experience. You need that to make proper judgments. Ideally, one would wish to have both—wisdom and innocence!

VON BOEHM: *Children often instinctively find the essence of something. I think that is what your architecture is all about . . . essence.*

PEI: It's hard to get to the essential. It's easier for a child. It's harder for us, we who have lived a life of contradictions. But I think it can be achieved. At least I try and I will keep on trying.

VON BOEHM: *Which principles did you apply in the education of your own children? Did you instill some values from your own upbringing or was that completely different?*

PEI: My father had always said this to me: "Education is the most important thing in your life. I will give you whatever you need to further your education." My father was not a rich man, but he had the means to support his children in this regard. I said the same thing to my children. I said the same thing to my grandchildren. It doesn't matter if they want to go to Harvard or Yale, I will help them. I want them to have that education, but they will have to work for it. My sons and my daughter all received the finest education that they wished to have.

VON BOEHM: *I think the most important is to find a kind of vision, to find an idea, to find out what you really want to do and what you are really good at. Did you help your children to find out?*

PEI: I did not point a way for them. I wanted them to find their way themselves. I provided them with the means to do what they wanted to do in education. What they wanted to be was entirely of their own volition. I might have had some influence on them. Sometimes it might have actually been negative. When two of my sons wanted to be architects, which is in fact what they are now, I was rather negative about it. I said that it is a rather difficult life. To be an architect you have to have a great love for the profession that you are entering into and success does not come early. It is an old man's business. You have to work for many years before you are recognized or given the opportunity to do work on your own. We are dealing with a fairly large investment of capital. People don't just choose a twenty-five year old to design an office building. A small house perhaps, if you are lucky.

VON BOEHM: *All the big projects take an average of thirteen years. So it really takes a while to become famous or at least well known.*

PEI: Yes, that's right. I said to my sons: "You must think very carefully before you decide to do this." I did not encourage them to study to become architects, nor did I discourage them. When they said that they wanted to, I said, "Alright then, go ahead."

VON BOEHM: *To see two sons in their own architectural firm and the other son in a related business . . . is that a source of satisfaction?*

PEI: It is a source of satisfaction, but I also worry about it because I am both a benefit to them and also a problem for them. Unavoidably if they do something very well someone will say, "Oh, your father did it." How can they be happy about that? I almost always went out of my way to explain to their clients to be sure that they leave me out of it. Of course it is difficult for them not to mention that they are sons of mine. On the other hand they have had opportunities that they otherwise might not have had without my being there. But I tried always to guarantee their freedom and independence.

VON BOEHM: *For you, a kind of architectural freedom started only when you were thirty-eight years old. The National Center for Atmospheric Research in Boulder, Colorado, was the first big challenge for you—at least aesthetically.*

PEI: Also to deal with nature, which is something I have great affinity for. I feel very comfortable with relating buildings to nature. It is second nature to me. If you ask me if there is anything from my background that comes out in my architecture, I would say no. If you talk about the relationship between nature and building, I would say yes. Maybe there is something like a kind of sensitivity to nature that I must have inherited just as you have inherited music in your very being. When that project came I was very enthusiastic. It was the first important project I undertook independent of Zeckendorf. That was in 1961.

VON BOEHM: *It was a very difficult site to start with, because first of all it was difficult to get there. Nature may have been inspiring, but in this case also brought about some severe restrictions.*

PEI: It was an awe-inspiring site at the foothills of the Rockies—they are the Alps of America. The problem was the overwhelming scale of the mountains in the background. It had to be a kind of building that could coexist with the powerful scale of nature. I had been working in cities all my life: this was a welcome change and a challenge. After having been given this project I decided to learn about the area. I rented a car, and my wife Eileen and I drove around parts of Colorado, Arizona, and New Mexico. I saw the Air Force Academy designed by Skidmore, Owings & Merrill at Colorado Springs, in a setting much like our own, but much more expansive. The buildings were very elegant, obviously inspired by Mies, with an aluminum and glass curtain wall. That was one of two possible approaches for the architect. Both acknowledge the power of the setting. This approach postulates that architecture is an object that is detached from nature. You see what I mean? It is on stilts, and appears to me at first glance to be a very logical approach. It is an approach that I could have taken, but I somehow felt uncomfortable about the relationship between the buildings and the setting. The buildings appeared too small. There is nothing you can ever do to be in scale with the mountains if the buildings are purposely detached from them. If you look at structures built by the Indians, like Mesa Verdes, they are like embedded rocks and rooted trees. So I chose the other approach. I wanted it to look as if it were carved out of the mountain.

VON BOEHM: *And when you look at the site from far away you don't even see that there is a building. And when you come closer it becomes a mountain on its own—with cubistic openings. It has very cubistic elements. And this contrast creates a movement, which then gives the impression of perfect harmony.*

PEI: Interesting that you say that. When I went there to explore the place I thought a lot about harmony. I recalled the places I had seen with my mother when I was a little boy—the mountaintop Buddhist retreats. There in the Colorado mountains, I tried to listen to the silence again—just as my mother had taught me. The investigation of the place became a kind of religious experience for me. And the project gave me the opportunity to break away from the Bauhaus approach. That exactly was my goal.

VON BOEHM: *And that is what later became a kind of trademark—even if you don't like to hear that—one might call it "meditative geometry."*

PEI: I think I can accept this expression. And the inspiration in this particular case really came from the Indians. The Indians have been there a long time; they worship nature and wish to coexist in harmony with it. I too wished to approach the design for NCAR in Boulder much the same way. I could not build with stone from the surrounding mountains like the Indians did, for it would have been prohibitively expensive. So we crushed the stone quarried from the mountains nearby and poured this aggregate into the concrete. Then we bush hammered the walls mechanically to reveal the aggregate, which harmonizes with the color of the mountain. From a distance the building blends into the foothills of the mountains.

VON BOEHM: *Like in a Cubist painting, where you don't have to have necessarily realistic colors. They can be different. And you get the best effects if they are just a little different. Here, they don't diverge from those of the physical world that surrounds the building. It reminds me of Cézanne's paintings.*

PEI: Mesa Verdes could have come out of a Cézanne painting, with its cubistic forms. The National Center for Atmospheric Research is a piece of cubistic work. I visited it recently and I found the approach was correct even though the architecture was a bit immature.

VON BOEHM: *It was not only a project about how to integrate a building into nature. There was something very important about the inner structure as well. The director, Walter Orr Roberts, was looking for interaction between the scientists, which is tremendously important for science. How could you translate that wish into architecture?*

PEI: The requirement for interaction with scientists was an opportunity that I welcomed. I would not have been able to create a building of those articulated forms were it not for their special requirements. They didn't want long corridors with numbers on the doors. They wanted to be individuals. That desire to be individuals is what made it possible for me to create those towers, because in each tower there are only three or four offices. The only way to get to those offices is not by elevator—they don't like elevators. (I don't know what will happen when they become old or handicapped.) Instead they have small circular stairs —they love the stairs. They call their offices the crow's nests, and they say they can think there. They say, "I don't have too many colleagues near me, as I like that feeling of isolation." Another requirement which worked to my advantage was that they wanted places for chance meetings. They say that some of their most creative moments are chance meetings in a place where they can get away from the traffic, see a good view, and have a good conversation. This is why the corridor is never straight. Where there is a good view it becomes wider so you can get away from the traffic and talk. We have a lot of those things that make it possible to give this group of buildings a bit of personality. The fact that it had a low budget was not something I regret. If I had had more money, I would have designed it the same way. Looking at it today, I can say that I was definitely influenced by Cubism in my architecture.

VON BOEHM: *You're also an art collector and you are interested in ancient Chinese art as well as in the classic modernists such as the cubists and sculptors/painters like Dubuffet and Giacometti. When did your interest in the arts start?*

PEI: Quite early I had already formulated certain notions about art and the relationship between art and architecture. I developed an interest in art quite early. (I'm not talking about Oriental art, I'm talking about Western art.) My first interest was Abstract Expressionism. My wife and I acquired a de Kooning and a Kline in the fifties. They are still with us. Architecture is an art form, there is no question about that. Not surprisingly, my interest in Cubism arose about the time when I sensed a certain symbiosis between it and architecture. Le Corbusier's work undoubtedly influenced me in that regard. Returning to art collection, I wish to state that I am not a real collector: I simply did not have the means or the time to be one. But I had some friends who helped me acquire some art. The few things I have today are all from friends—Jean Dubuffet, Jacques Lipchitz, Henry Moore, Zao Wou-Ki, and Barnett Newman. My interest in Western art started back in the forties. My wife and I used to spend our Saturday afternoons going from gallery to gallery. We don't do that now. In fact it is probably because of that that I got to know your friend Pierre Matisse.

VON BOEHM: *Who was one of New York's most eminent art dealers and the son of Henri Matisse. He had made artists like Chagall, Giacometti and Miró known to the American public.*

PEI: He had a wonderful gallery on 57th Street since the late twenties and I would go in and look at all the exhibitions. I couldn't afford to buy Giacometti or Dubuffet, whose work he was showing at that time. I wish I had because in those years they were very inexpensive. I found that Pierre had a wonderful eye and he always chose not only the best artist, but also the best work of that artist. So I visited that gallery more than any others. He was very generous. He would take me into the storehouse and show me things. After all he didn't have to, and he knew I wouldn't be able to buy it, I couldn't afford to buy it, but he spent time with me. He took me in and said, "Are you interested in Giacometti? I'll show you some more works of his." Then he took me inside the storeroom and showed me more. The early Dubuffets were not at all appealing to me. They were very brutal and primitive to the untrained eye. It was Pierre who opened my eyes. It is through him that I became interested in Dubuffet. Years later I made his acquaintance and we became very good friends. Every time my wife and I went to Paris, we would visit him and his wife Lili. The same with many other artists.

VON BOEHM: *What did you admire in Dubuffet? I tend to think that you and he were very different.*

PEI: We were quite different. I found him very stimulating because he saw the world with a unique vision. He despised "culture." He believed there was beauty in l'art brut. I admired him because he developed a personal language of art. Once you understand that language, then you can understand his art. The time that I became absolutely committed to his work was, I think, in 1964. I saw a retrospective exhibition of his work at the Palazzo Gritti in Venice. There, when I was able to see the panorama of his work, I acquired a certain knowledge of that language. One thing is sure: I cannot imagine my life without the arts, without sculpture and painting.

VON BOEHM: *And it has become a very important part of your life to design the right space for works of art. The process starts—as always—with the analysis of a space. Let's take the example of the National Gallery, the East Wing, which is probably a very good example to analyze because it was almost an impossible site— is there an example in the history of architecture where you have this sharp triangular space? Could you try to describe the way of analyzing a problem using the example of the East Wing?*

PEI: The site was not my first concern. I guess my first concern really was the fact that it was on the great Mall of Washington, D.C. I was more concerned about symbolism than almost anything else. This was to be a very public building located in the most public of places. This building had to relate to the other public buildings whose ensemble was first planned by L'Enfant in 1789 and elaborated by McMillan in 1900. I felt that the new building needed to relate to the existing ensemble, especially to the West Wing by John Russell Pope. This is not unlike relationships among people in a community. Equally important, to my mind, it had to be an architecture of its time. Maybe it is the Chinese in me to give such deference to harmony: it is due to a belief that this is a place where the whole is greater than its parts.

As a building, the East Building was designed to complement the West Building to make the whole a better functioning modern museum. For example, there is almost no

I.M. Pei's sketch showing
the East Building on axis
with the West Building and
aligned with the diagonal of
Pennsylvania Avenue

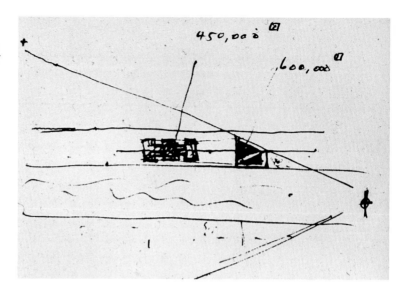

basement in the first building. It has inadequate storage fa-
cilities, and almost no space for conservation: it was designed as a monument. The new building needed to make
up for these deficiencies. But that was only the beginning.
It had to accommodate an ever-increasing collection of
modern art. Today's museums are more than places solely
for the permanent exhibition of masterpieces of the past. In
order to stay active and alive, they have to have temporary
galleries for changing exhibitions. The new building was
designed with that in mind. In 1978 when it was opened, it
exhibited "The Treasures of Dresden," which attracted an
attendance of 620,000. At this moment, more than twenty
years later, it is exhibiting "The Golden Age of Chinese Ar-
chaeology." To accommodate these large attendances, we
designed a glass-enclosed piazza for all seasons. I am told
that it is one of the most popular gathering places in Washington.

So far I have talked only about the exhibition portions
of the East Building. Attached to it to the south is a triangular wing, which contains new administrative offices,
a study and research center for the visual arts, a library,
a cafe, and storage for one of the largest collections of the
graphic arts.

VON BOEHM: *What was the source for the garden? Can we
say that you went back to your childhood for inspiration? It
also reminds me of churches, actually. There is just more than
in a church.*

PEI: I wanted the atrium garden to be a life-giving force. I remember in the early years we frequently took our children to visit museums on weekends. The Metropolitan has a wonderful collection, but they never liked it. They loved the Guggenheim. They loved the huge void in the middle and the snail-like ramp on which they could run around. I wanted to create the same kind of attraction for children that the Guggenheim had. I am not belittling the importance of providing an attractive environment to display the collection to the art-loving public. It is just that today's museum must pay greater attention to its educational responsibility, especially to the young.

VON BOEHM: *Actually, you were facing quite a contradiction: the strategic position on the Mall called for greatness, whereas for a museum smallness can actually be crucial—the human scale that children sense even more then grown-ups. All too often in museums, people are overwhelmed by architecture, neo-classical architecture, or they simply suffer from museum fatigue, which is what we all know when we get completely tired after one hour. We have to walk very long corridors. In contrast, in the National Gallery I feel a sort of a human scale. Was this part of your concept from the beginning and how did you achieve that?*

PEI: It was not a conscious attempt on my part. It was probably very natural for me to be aware of the importance of human scale. Most public buildings designed in neo-classical style are a little bit intimidating.

Look at all the memorials in Washington: they all have impressively big spaces to glorify an idea or a person. But art museums are not memorials. They should be designed

I.M. Pei's sketch showing the East Building of the National Gallery on the Mall in Washington, D.C.

to attract the public to come for sheer enjoyment. This helps the museum to achieve its chief mission, i.e., to exhibit the best in art and thus to enlighten the public, young and old, to the importance of art in their lives.

VON BOEHM: *But still there remained the contradiction between the creation of something great, which was definitely expected in the capital of the United States, the wish for a house-like museum, and the regulations on height, among others. How did you finally solve these problems?*

PEI: Sometimes there exists an opportunity when you can solve two or three problems at the same time. The biggest challenge for us was to accommodate the rules and regulations of Washington, which is, of course, in the District of Columbia. Our site is located at the intersection of two avenues: Pennsylvania and Constitution. These two important avenues have different height limitations. We had to accommodate both, and that was very difficult indeed. Carter Brown and I both wished to reduce the scale, both physically and functionally, of the East Building. I thought that by varying the heights of the building,

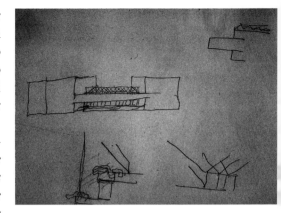
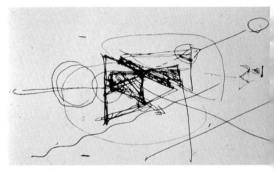
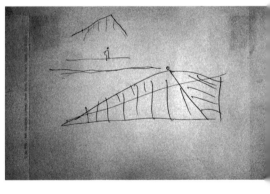

Sketches by I.M. Pei showing the development of the geometric basis of the East Building

we could accommodate the height regulations on the one hand and create three small three-story towers at the same time, to become three "house museums" for different exhibitions. Or, if the occasion arises, they can be interconnected to accommodate one larger exhibition. The "house museum" idea occurred to us after we visited the Poldi Pezzoli in Milan in 1970. It has a stair that connects three levels. It has a human scale rarely found in museums. By incorporating this idea into the East Building, we reduced the scale of a large museum and at the same time increased flexibility.

VON BOEHM: *Why is it that we get a feeling of a small scale and an incredible rhythm in a space that is split into many triangular spaces? Maybe it is the different vanishing points . . . it is a rhythm that you create by geometry.*

PEI: The site is a triangle. In the beginning I felt very uneasy about it. I felt that there was a restriction which I was obliged to overcome. Sometimes when you are trying to solve a problem, you may hit on an idea that turns the problem into an asset. That idea had to do with perspective. I had visited many great buildings, especially in Europe, which taught me the lesson of movement and perspective. The Basilica of St. Peter's in Rome is a strongly axial building. You walk down the nave and you approach the baldachino and you go beyond it to the altar. That movement is very impressive; it is almost intimidating. This movement along a single vanishing point perspective is intentional, to impress upon one the authority of the church. Then I remember, many years later, I went to Germany and Austria: Vienna, Salzburg, and Linz. I saw churches that were very different. Some I found were much more human, and not so impressive as St. Peter's. They were influenced by Italian Baroque, and were designed for a very different purpose: to celebrate life. Instead of keeping light away, they brought light in. The most convincing example is the church I found last, a pilgrimage church called Vierzehnheiligen, in southern Germany. There I found the sensuality of church design, the voluptuousness of it. I walked into that church and had an entirely different feeling. St. Peter's and that relatively small pilgrimage church—they were both serving the same religion, Christianity, yet one was so very different from the other. At that moment I didn't know what it meant. But when I was confronted with the triangle, I thought of the church in Germany. Why is it that these Baroque churches are so sensual whereas St. Peter's is so intimidating? It was not all the plasterwork,

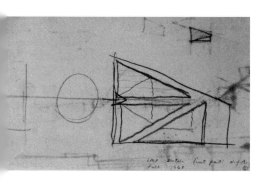
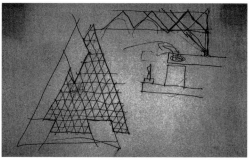

which is very beautiful. What was the secret? I think the secret was in the curvilinear surfaces found in those churches, which were the direct descendants of Borromini, animated by ever-changing light.

VON BOEHM: *Why do curves create sensuality? We know that curves in the human body are very important. In architectural forms, what makes a curve different, and what makes your pilgrimage church different from St. Peter's?*

PEI: St. Peter's was designed with single-point perspective. You can draw it with all the lines converging on a single vanishing point. Curvilinear surfaces, on the other hand, have endless points. When you move in such a space, the perspective changes constantly. Most buildings are designed with an orthogonal grid that has only two vanishing points. A triangular grid on the other hand has three. It was this lesson that taught me to turn the constraint of the triangle into an asset. When one moves through the atrium garden, the changes in perspective enrich the visual perception of the space.

VON BOEHM: *I think there is no other museum in the United States of America that attracts so many people as a building. If you look at the sharp angle on the outside you know that it is almost no longer there because people like to touch it. Once in their lifetime they want to touch this sharp angle.*

PEI: I still don't know why. After the first few months since the opening, that sharp corner you mentioned became stained by the touch of hands. Being an architect who wishes to protect his architecture, I asked the contractor, who was still there at the time to sandblast it. They did. Two or three months later the same thing happened again, and after a while I gave up. I think people are attracted to something they have not experienced before, the sharp point. I insisted on it but I didn't know why. Maybe I too find that the knife edge sharpness of stone is very enticing.

VON BOEHM: *I think people want to touch it because they think it can't be stable. It is so fine and thin and the angle is so sharp that it looks unstable. It is something almost from another world for them, because they have never seen it before. Yet there it is.*

PEI: The reason why they had never seen it before is because the stone companies would discourage you from doing it. They say that it will break. I said perhaps yes or perhaps not, but it would be exciting if we could get it built.

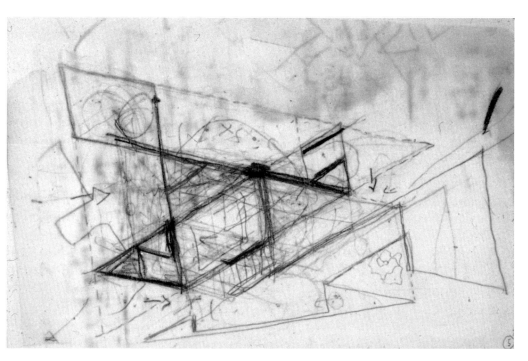

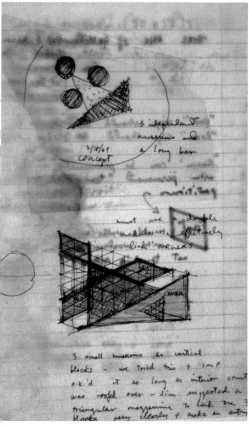

2/18/61
concept

3 independent
museums and
a long bar

must use a double
saddlers... effectively
"link" corners
so

CENTER

3 small museums as vertical
blocks — we tried this + I.M.P.
o.k.'d it so long as interior court
was roofed over — Jim suggested a
triangular mezzanine to link the 3
blocks very clearly + make an entry

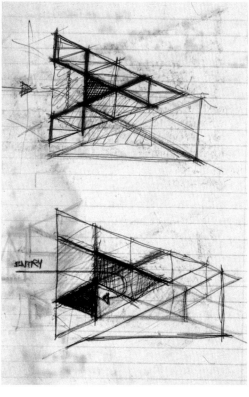

ENTRY

The growth of the design into architecture with legible
parts, sketched by I.M. Pei

My client did not object to it. They let me do it. I think to-day no one would want to change it.

VON BOEHM: *And one would never want to change the Henry Moore sculpture at the entrance. This has a little history to it as well. I think at first you wanted to see the sculpture on the Pennsylvania Avenue side of the building.*

PEI: I do recall that. To commission public art is something I support, but it should be done in collaboration with the artist, especially with regard to scale and siting. The question was to whom should we give the commission. I think there were three artists mentioned by Carter Brown at that time. Of course he had a very strong opinion himself: he was the director of the museum. He mentioned that Henry Moore should be on the list. Then I asked, "What about Dubuffet?"

We discussed this in a board meeting, and no one was able to decide between Dubuffet and Moore. Carter and I said, "Why don't we go and visit the two of them, or better yet invite them to come here." I think we invited Henry Moore. He selected a piece of sculpture that was like a spindle (I have forgotten the name now), like one of those tops which you play with as a child, with string. He didn't specify where to put it, but he specified that object. I did not think it was one of his best pieces. Carter said, "Alright, we will talk to Henry and see if we can find something else," because at that time Mr. Moore rarely made a sculpture specifically for a place. He preferred to select one of his many maquettes and enlarge it to a scale appropriate to the setting. He was very practical in that regard.

VON BOEHM: *Did you invite Dubuffet as well?*

PEI: He was my recommendation. It was out of courtesy to me that he was included. We invited him to come, as he was in New York at that time. I went down to Washington with him and took him to see the big maquette of the proposed East Building. He asked for some tin foil. So we brought him the tin foil and he started to make half a dozen scale figures and put them in front of the maquette. I found them very interesting in an abstract sort of way. We asked if he would be interested in the project. He said "Yes, you come to Paris in a few months and I will show you something." As soon as he was ready, Carter and I went to his studio in Vincennes. He had made the maquettes of five strange-looking figures of people in red, white, and blue, with black outlines. He made an opening to simulate the entrance of the East Building, and put his figures in it like on a stage. He called it "the welcome parade." This whimsical piece seemed to me to complement the building in a very interesting way.

VON BOEHM: *It was kind of a twinkle in the eye.*

PEI: It has a whimsical sense of humor. I thought the building needed that light touch. Carter was not so sure.

VON BOEHM: *Too risky, maybe.*

PEI: He told me very honestly, "You know, the East Building may be paid for by the Mellons, but the annual support and maintenance will be by Congress. Some of its members may not be comfortable with this kind of art." I knew he was right, and I did not push too much more. Did I tell Dubuffet that? I don't remember.

Henry Moore is a different story. He stopped over at Washington en route to Dallas. We showed him our recommended placement on the Pennsylvania Avenue side of the building. He not only rejected it, but was angry with me for having suggested it. To him, sculpture must have sun to bring it to light. The northeasterly placement was simply unacceptable. Of course, he was absolutely right.

VON BOEHM: *For him sculpture was like a living being, and every little change of light meant a lot to him. If a sculpture at a particular location didn't catch the right light it was dead, and therefore the location was impossible.*

PEI: Yes, I knew that I was wrong to suggest that location. I quickly turned around and offered him the entrance of the National Gallery. He loved it. He had light.

VON BOEHM: *It is beautiful how the light plays with the metal, and how the color is so different at different times of the day as the light changes. And the light creates beautiful reflections.*

PEI: I chose that piece. I chose it because the name of that piece is *Knife-edge*. It is very appropriate for this building, for it has a knife-edge of its own.

VON BOEHM: *Do you still say that this is one of the three most important buildings that you've done, if you had a hierarchy of buildings?*

PEI: I certainly would. It was important at that time because America was so much looking forward to finding a modern solution to a public building of this nature. It was not easy to do it. This building was immediately accepted by the public and the architectural profession. The critiques that came were so unanimous that I was worried. It couldn't be that good. It worried me. It wasn't. It was a serious attempt. Since then symbolism became a little less of a concern for American architecture. In terms of creating a building symbolically appropriate to this time, place and purpose, I think I would consider the building as a sort of success. Architecturally there are lots of faults. I know more about them than others. I don't mean the execution —the execution is very good, everything about it. What I mean is rather the formal awkwardness, which I noticed but couldn't do anything to alter. There are constraints that I must follow, like height limits. Or the fact that a museum is a museum, which has lots of walls . . . blank walls. It is also difficult because there is only one street to enter. I had two entrances: one to the center, the research center, and one to the public area. It was very difficult to solve the axial problem and the double entrance from the same street. I was not allowed to have the entrance on the Mall and I was not permitted to have the entrance on Pennsylvania Avenue because of the triangle. So I had one street and two entrances. One is more important than the other, but the less important one cannot be unimportant. That was a difficulty, but it was solved to my satisfaction. The forms were a little awkward. I couldn't do better within the confines and limitations. I don't think I have ever succeeded in satisfying myself in any project. It is always the case that something could be better.

VON BOEHM: *The example of the National Gallery shows that analysis is not everything but is still the foundation of everything. Can you give some general rules that you follow that constitute your way to analyze a problem?*

PEI: Time, place, and purpose are the three priorities that demand careful analysis in the search for a solution for a particular project. Also important are budgetary, technical, and formal concerns, which come later. The solution is the result of a balancing act, trying to satisfy all those demands, though not necessarily in equal measure.

VON BOEHM: *The measure can even vary in the course of the project. But are the younger architects today actually prepared for that? Aren't they rather looking for a possibility to put their own signature on a building instead of completely serving the purpose and adding a kind of signature to that if possible?*

PEI: That is why I say that if one were to have a very strict stylistic approach to architecture—how much would be missed? A piece of architecture is the embodiment of a combination of factors, i.e. time, place, and use. To put it another way, it is the *where*, the *when*, and the *why* that a work must address, convincingly and eloquently and with style. To me that is the heart of architecture. Over-emphasis on style at the expense of the other concerns would limit the untapped richness of possibilities in a work of architecture. I would like to cite two examples to show that just the difference in site (place) alone can make a big difference in the approach to design. One is the Miho Museum and the other is the National Center for Atmospheric Research in Boulder. How very different they are! The differences make them interesting for me because in these cases it is not really the difference in function or use; I think the important difference here is site. When you compare the Japanese landscape to the Rocky Mountains, there is a huge contrast. So therefore how can I apply just one style? That is why the Skidmore, Owings & Merrill building in Colorado Springs, the Air Force Academy, is stylistic. Right away it says Mies van der Rohe. I want to ask you, could I have put the NCAR building in Boulder on the Shigaraki Mountains in Japan?

VON BOEHM: *Honestly, I don't think so, because the muscularity of NCAR matches the muscularity of the Rocky Mountains, and I couldn't imagine it in any other place.*

PEI: Exactly. And the design of the Miho building was influenced by the landscape of that part of Japan. I find that I am not missing anything from so-called restrictions.

I found I was having more fun trying to explore the possibilities of adapting the building to the nature of the place, rather than being restricted by a preconceived notion of what my building should look like stylistically. Yes, and I think that it is therefore a kind of responsibility not to insist too much on a signature which the public can recognize. Instead, I am all for exploring the possibilities inherent in the project.

VON BOEHM: *Is there a dialogue today in architecture about these things? Do you exchange such ideas with your colleagues worldwide?*

PEI: I wish there were more dialogue. But there isn't really. Of course there are symposiums and congresses, but what are they good for? They are all about theory—people put it on paper afterwards and it is soon forgotten. After I did the Miho Museum in Japan, I would love to have had a real dialogue with the Japanese architects whom I admire. I would have been tremendously interested in their reaction. But much to my regret that did not happen.

VON BOEHM: *Do you think they are denying their roots in a way?*

PEI: In a way, that could be. I ask this question all the time when I look at their buildings, many of which I like very much. I gave a talk recently at Tokyo University at the invitation of Tadao Ando. He introduced me to the Dean, who introduced my work to the audience but never mentioned Miho. I didn't ask why. I have two explanations —I don't know which is the right one—maybe it is a combination of the two. One is that the client is a spiritual organization and they are very leery of spiritual organizations. The other explanation is that I had taken an approach they don't agree with but at the same time are challenged by.

VON BOEHM: *Maybe their not mentioning Miho is not a judgment; perhaps they are just timid. That is also a Japanese attitude. They don't want to comment on it.*

PEI: It did puzzle me then and it continues to puzzle me now. I would expect the students to ask questions such as, "Why does this building look so Japanese? Is it right? Have we not moved on to a more global approach to architecture?" Those kinds of questions would have been interesting. We would have had an interesting dialogue on that subject. They asked me about the Louvre and the National Gallery but they never asked me about the Miho Museum.

VON BOEHM: *They may not be so interested in their own country. This is a phenomenon you have in architecture world-wide today. Look at yourself. When have you done a building in the United States lately? Rather, you have designed for France, Germany, Japan, China . . .*

PEI: For me, it is because I was offered those wonderful opportunities abroad—exactly the things I wanted to do. One would have to analyze why these offers didn't come in the United States—there are various reasons, and also coincidences play a role here. But in general it is a sign of our age that most architects in the world today, and not just in America, are going further and further away from the past, which perhaps they consider irrelevant. In my opinion, the future has its roots in the past. History is not only relevant, it is essential to the creation of the new.

VON BOEHM: *I understand very well.*

PEI: It is not a question of my being defensive. I strongly believe that history is a continuum and architecture needs to flow with it. There are new possibilities which I would like to explore in the next ten years of work. I look forward to this very much.

VON BOEHM: *Where would you put your emphasis? Or what would be your new possibilities?*

PEI: I would like to be more experimental. I think I know in which direction I can go to explore a little more deeply into the past to search for answers that satisfy the spiritual side of architecture.

VON BOEHM: *Would you be more experimental with materials or with forms?*

PEI: It would always be forms and space; materials to me are secondary. When you have the right form, a material can be found to create it. So technology is not my principal concern. The fewer constraints one has, the more experimental one can be.

Grand Louvre, Phase I, Paris, 1983–89 (rendering by Paul Stevenson Oles)

The Challenge of the Louvre

VON BOEHM: *What was your impression of the Louvre when you first came to Paris after they had asked you to think about the giant project of the "Grand Louvre"? I think before you accepted the project you visited the museum three times secretly.*

PEI: Yes, I think that was in 1983. One of my conditions prior to accepting the commission was to learn as much as I could about the Louvre. Of course, I knew the museum and the whole complex from earlier visits to Paris. But now I wanted to see if there was something I could do, because if I found it impossible for me to make a contribution, I would have to say no. But after three secret "private" visits, I came to the conclusion that something could be done and must be done. It wasn't difficult to discover that the Louvre was totally unworkable. The Louvre was built in parts successively since the 12th century, first as a *donjon*, then as a palace. So there you are . . . we have the problem of how to make a palace into a modern museum. The Louvre had lots of exhibition space on a palatial scale, but was totally lacking in infrastructure, such as space for mechanical equipment, for storage of paintings and other art objects, for an auditorium, restaurants, cafés, shops, and things of that kind. After some thought I decided that there was indeed something that one could do. So I said to myself, "Yes, I am going to try."

VON BOEHM: *One of the best examples of what has been achieved with the Louvre is not so much the pyramid. It is rather the change that has occurred in the courtyards. I remember the condition in which you found the courtyards in the Richelieu wing—and now they house sculptures, beautifully lighted through glass roofs.*

PEI: That came much later. Before 1989, the Louvre, the museum, was lopsided on the Seine side. Its main entry was at the Pavillon Denon. So it was quite some time before we attacked the problem of Pavillon Richelieu. The Richelieu Wing at that time belonged to the Ministry of Finance and Economy. In 1986, the Socialist Party lost the election and the then Minister did not want to move. That was quite clear. President Mitterrand did everything he could to make sure that the Ministry would move to their newly constructed building in Bercy. The Richelieu Wing was critical to the realization of the Grand Louvre, as it is called today. Cour Marly used to be a "Cour d'Honneur" for the Minister; cars were parked there. It was a waste of space as far as the museum was concerned.

In a 1984 meeting at Arcachon, I proposed to cover this court as well as the adjacent court, which was used to service the Ministry. By covering those courts with glass roofs, with very little effort we obtained a tremendous amount of exhibition space which would be ideal for sculpture. The Chevaux de Marly that you see there now used to be on the Place de la Concorde. It was quite obvious that sooner or later they were going to disintegrate. So they wanted to put them indoors, and that is why the conservator of sculpture at the Louvre liked the idea of the two large glass-enclosed courts. I did not realize until much later that we won the support of the Museum conservators on that day in Arcachon. Emile Biasini should be credited for calling the meeting at that seaside town in the middle of winter.

VON BOEHM: *What has the Louvre become for Paris now in terms of its position in the city?*

PEI: In 1983 the Louvre was a barrier. The heterogeneous collection of bushes and trees in the Cour Napoléon made it unsafe to use it, especially at night. We proposed transforming the Cour from a barrier into a point of attraction. Another key to opening up the Louvre to the city, urbanistically speaking, is the Richelieu Wing. The Richelieu Wing and the Passage Richelieu were entirely occupied by the Ministry of Economy and Finance and were closed to the public. We proposed to open it up. Once the Passage was opened, the Louvre became a safe and attractive connector of the left and right banks of the Seine.

VON BOEHM: *What is this project for you, now that it is finally completed? What is it in your life, for you personally?*

PEI: After the Louvre, you would think that everything would be less exciting. It need not be, no, it need not be. The Louvre is a challenge that you get only once in a lifetime. And it took thirteen years to finish the Louvre project, from beginning to end. And I don't think I would want

Grand Louvre, renderings
of the exterior and interior
(by Paul Stevenson Oles)

The Challenge of the Louvre   79

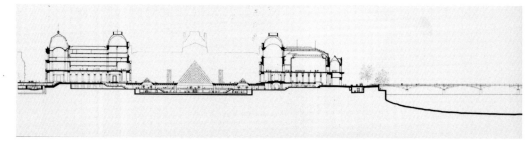

to do another Louvre. The Grand Louvre was difficult from the beginning. We had our critics at the outset. My guess is that maybe 90 percent of the people of Paris were opposed to the project in the beginning. This wasn't surprising, because the Louvre is a national monument, and people liked it the way it was. And when we introduced the idea of a pyramid, that was the limit, the polemics reached a crescendo in 1984–85, and I received many angry glances in the streets of Paris. But looking back at it now, it all becomes rather pleasurable, because they look at me differently now. That means they have accepted Le Grand Louvre. I like that.

VON BOEHM: *Why is that? Why does it take some time for people to get used to architecture? Why first the opposition and now almost everybody loves it, except for some hardliners?*

PEI: Well, architecture has an attribute that I find extremely interesting: architecture is something that an individual can very quickly understand. It is the opposite of Einstein's theory of relativity. You know, someone can explain that to me over and over again and I will not understand it, but architecture is something that everybody can understand, after it is built. Once they inhabit it, they know, "Ah yes, it works well. Now I see." So it is not so difficult for people to accept it once it is built. The difficulty is to get it built. That I think is the challenge. I would say the support of a few people in this case can make a tremendous difference. It goes without saying that President Mitterrand was far and above the most important supporter, and then Emile Biasini, who navigated the political whirlpool with great determination and finesse.

VON BOEHM: *One tends to think that architecture has to do mostly with calculations, with geometry, with mathematics. But I think it has a lot to do with emotions and with physical feelings—with the senses. Do you agree?*

PEI: Yes, I think when you talk about space and volume, you can't help but think about it as a work of geometry. The emotional response you mentioned is intensified by the modulation of light and the movement of people in that space. Those two ingredients are essential to architecture. It is not just volume and space alone.

VON BOEHM: *How did you solve the problem of the lack of space for infrastructure, storage, and the technical necessities? Was that complex, and what finally was the solution?*

PEI: The Louvre was begun in the 12th century as a *donjon*, or fortress, for soldiers, food and ammunition, for the defense of the Ile de la Cité. Over the centuries, the structure was added to several times, and it became a palace where the royal family lived. Later, various kings exhibited their art there, but it was not until the time of Napoléon that the Louvre was seriously considered a public museum. And in modern times, though used as a museum, it never had the infrastructure necessary for this function. When I was brought in, in 1983, I determined to solve this problem. It wasn't possible to find the necessary space in the building itself, because one didn't want to

Grand Louvre, rendering of the interior space (by Paul Stevenson Oles)

demolish the wonderful rooms of the Louvre.

VON BOEHM: *The only solution was to find the room underground for storage and infrastructure. You had to excavate.*

PEI: Yes, the only solution was to excavate the two courtyards, the Cour Carrée and the Cour Napoléon. Before you undertake an excavation you have to know what is underground. The Cour Carrée

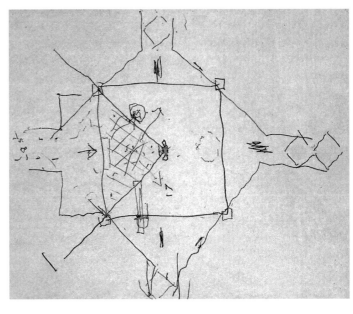

I.M. Pei's sketch for the Grand Louvre, Pyramide

is in the oldest part of the Louvre, where the *donjon* is. There is nothing you could do with it except unearth it and preserve it.

But the Cour Napoléon presented us with an opportunity. We looked at the old archaeological drawings: the archaeologists we consulted were quite confident about the accuracy of these drawings. The excavation that followed proved them to be correct. Fortunately, under the Cour Napoléon there was nothing of great historical importance. The meticulous excavation of the two courtyards took more than a year, and convinced us that we could safely proceed with our recommendations. Otherwise, the whole project could very well have been stopped right there.

VON BOEHM: *I think the proposal for excavation was accepted quite easily by the authorities, so that you could present the idea to François Mitterrand, who had asked you to do the project.*

PEI: In 1984 I told the President, "There is one step that must be taken to give the museum the kind of infrastructure support it needs. The only feasible solution is to excavate the Cour Napoléon to the level of the Seine, and create two new underground levels to provide all the infrastructure that a great museum like the Louvre should have." He replied, "Très bien." I believe he must have consulted others on that subject. His unhesitating "Très bien" to my recommendation continues to amaze me to this day. I am convinced that if the Cour Napoléon had not been excavated there would have been no solution, and Le Grand Louvre could not be what it has become today.

VON BOEHM: *If nothing had happened, the Louvre itself, as a museum, would be almost dead now. There would still be a barrier between the two sides of the Seine. And the dark, monumental buildings themselves would still scare off many people. It was not inviting at all. What it needed—as much as a new storage area and infrastructure—was an inviting entrance area. How did the idea of the pyramid actually come about? In the beginning and even later you were accused of designing an Egyptian death symbol. The pyramid plays a role in many different cultures, including your native China. Is it a symbol at all for you, or was it just a matter, again, of analysis?*

PEI: The glass pyramid is a symbol that defines the entry to the Louvre. It is placed precisely at the center of gravity of the three pavilions. There were many thoughtful people, such as Michel Guy, who would have preferred multiple entries to break up the Louvre into several museums. In my opinion, that would have created total confusion in the minds of the visiting public. A large, multi-discipline museum such as the Louvre needs a central point of arrival for the general public. For art specialists with very specific interests, arrangements could always be made in advance to avoid the ever-increasing number of museum visitors. For the general public, a main entry, though not necessarily the only entry, is mandatory. The pyramid assumes the func-

Plan, Pyramide

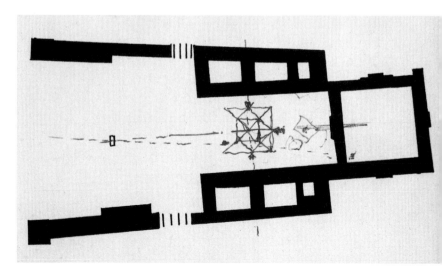

tion of a symbolic entry to a huge complex of meandering interconnected buildings which had no center.

The scale and nature of such a pyramid concerned us from the very beginning. It needed to be prominent enough to be the focus of this complex without compromising its authenticity as a national monument.

VON BOEHM: *Honestly, there are beautiful cathedrals with much better and much more interesting architecture than the Louvre.*

PEI: I agree, but it is the combination of many things that makes the Louvre so important. Without a doubt, as a work of architecture, the Louvre cannot be compared with the Cistercian Abbey of Le Thoronet or the Gothic cathedral of Chartres. But for eight hundred years the history of France was embedded in the stones of the Louvre. Not unimportant is the fact that the Louvre is located in the heart of Paris.

First of all, I was emboldened by Mitterrand's decision to move the Ministry of Finance out of the Louvre, to Bercy. With this move, the center of gravity of the future Louvre Museum would move to the center of the Cour Napoléon, which is where I located the pyramid. But anything done there has to be discreet and compatible with the Louvre.

VON BOEHM: *For me, now that the pyramid is there, I understand the Louvre and the architecture of it much better because I see the contrast.*

PEI: Part of the intention is exactly that. I am very pleased that you made such an observation. I decided that it had to be a symbol. The Louvre is now a museum, and no longer a palace for the kings of France. It is a museum for the "grand public," as the French would say.

VON BOEHM: *You could have said that the Louvre is a Baroque building, so why don't we put a cylinder or a cone in the middle to add to it yet another round shape? Why, instead, was a pyramid the result of your analysis?*

PEI: Why a pyramid? Well, we tried many other forms. We settled on a pyramid for a number of reasons. Formally, it is the most compatible with the architecture of the Louvre, especially with the faceted planes of its roofs. It is also one of the most structurally stable of forms, which assures its transparency, a major design objective. As it is constructed of glass and steel, it signifies a break with the architectural traditions of the past. It is a work of our time.

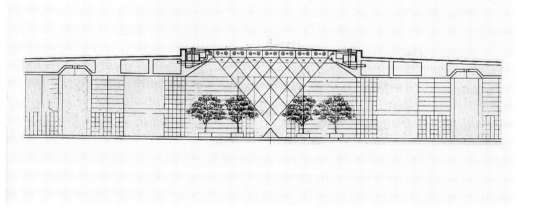

Pyramide Inversée,
photograph and section

VON BOEHM: *If it were solid and made of stone, it would be unapproachable, closed, a closed world. The glass structure, on the contrary, opens the world—the underground world and the building itself. If you stand under the pyramid and look at the Louvre through the geometric metal structure which holds the glass, you understand the architecture of the Baroque buildings.*

Were there other reasons for the pyramid form?

PEI: Other reasons? It was not because of Napoléon's Egyptian campaign, which made such a deep impression on the French. You are right to observe that the Egyptian pyramids were built of stone. I myself reminded my critics that there is no relation between a stone pyramid and our glass pyramid; one is constructed for the dead and the other for the living.

VON BOEHM: *Of course there was a lot of opposition. What was your strategy to convert people? How did you convert public figures like Madame Pompidou and Catherine Deneuve?*

PEI: Mme. Pompidou, Catherine Deneuve, and Pierre Boulez were among my few supporters. As I mentioned earlier, in 1984–85 most Parisians were against the project. The most articulate critic was M. Michel Guy, who was the Minister of Culture in President Pompidou's administration. Also, three art critics published a best-selling book (*Paris Mystifié*) condemning our design for converting the venerable Louvre into an art emporium (my word) catering to the public, who have little interest in "art." Mme. Pompidou with her experience at the Centre Pompidou understood the importance of exposing art to as large a public as possible. Mme. Deneuve, the great French actress, could not possibly have considered her work in film as purely an elitist undertaking. I believe they agreed with me that this museum, with its great art collection, should be open to all. To quote Malraux, "to make the outstanding works of humanity accessible to the greatest number of people."

VON BOEHM: *You could also have mentioned the fear of "American mass culture," because this was also an argument as far as I recall. And despite Mitterrand's enthusiasm there were a lot of protests. The Commission Superieure des Monuments Historiques gave you the hardest time on January 23, 1984. Just recently I had a chance to look at the minutes of that meeting, which was really quite wild. It was at that meeting that they called the scheme a gigantic ruined gadget and said that it was beyond their comprehension. When you tried to explain that the pyramid would look like a sparkling diamond with all the reflections of light, they said, "No, Mr. Pei, it will look awful, like a fake diamond and very cheap." Fortunately, you didn't understand all that.*

PEI: Oh no. My knowledge of French was fortunately limited. I would have left the room had I understood what they were saying. The person who translated for me was in tears. She so much wanted to defend me against their insulting arguments. They wanted to kill the project then and there. They almost succeeded.

VON BOEHM: *And you know that rejection has a history with the Louvre. We have to remember that François Mansart developed fifteen schemes for Louis XIV, three hundred years ago, to redesign the Louvre. They were all rejected. Then Ber-*

nini came and it was a fiasco. He was sent back to Italy in much disgrace.

PEI: But with much gold! The French architects were unanimously organized against Bernini. Colbert, Louis XIV's minister, sent him back to Italy. When I was fighting for my concept I often thought of that story about Bernini. Fortunately, Mitterrand had promised me in private that what happened to Bernini would not happen to me. In retrospect, the reason we succeeded has a lot to do with timing. What amazes me about the Louvre is its continuity. During its eight-hundred-year history it underwent changes rather infrequently and only for important social or political reasons. Le Grand Louvre became a reality not because of the logic of the plan but because President Mitterrand understood that Louvre the Palace, a complex of multiple and conflicting uses, should become, in its totality, Louvre the Museum.

VON BOEHM: *One crucial figure for the whole project as it proceeded was Jacques Chirac, then Mayor of Paris. He was not in favor of it and he made the special request to see the pyramid in full size before it was built.*

PEI: A meeting was arranged for me to explain the design to Chirac. I went to the Hôtel de Ville. Chirac was very friendly to me. That was unexpected. He didn't ask me anything about the pyramid. He talked about China, his experiences there, his interest in Chinese art, and for half an hour he took me around to look at the Chinese objects he had collected. At the end of this chitchat, he got up and said, "The press is waiting. Let's go" in English for my sake. He took me to meet the press. The *maquette* was there. For half an hour he lectured the press about the planning of Paris. He supported the design. He said that it was actually good for Paris urbanistically because it would open up Paris. When it came to the pyramid he was not so sure.

The next day the headlines quoted him, "I like the design of the whole project from an urbanistic point of view. But I am not sure about the pyramid, the size and the proportions. I would demand a full scale mock-up. Then everybody can form an impression of the pyramid. Historically, a *maquette grandeur* is frequently erected on-site prior to the construction of an important public project."

VON BOEHM: *There is a long history of such trial constructions. Napoléon did it for the Arc de Triomphe. And it was just recently done for the Stadtschloss in Berlin.*

PEI: The press said that Chirac was right. Because of time constraints, someone proposed the idea of using a crane to suspend four cables forming a full-size pyramid. I will never forget that day. I was flying back from the Orient and my plane was delayed. I didn't get there in time, but it didn't matter. Chirac looked at the form delineated by the cables and said "Not bad," and walked away. That was the turning point. From that point on criticism started to die down. I think the battle of the pyramid lasted about eighteen months. It was Chirac's acceptance of the *maquette* that had been crucial. It was the turning point.

VON BOEHM: *Now the pyramid is always mentioned along with the Tour Eiffel as a symbol of Paris. It is an emblem. Do you see that as a compliment?*

PEI: Of course that is a compliment. Unlike the Eiffel Tower, one does not see the pyramid on the skyline: one has to enter the Cour Napoléon to see it. One can see the Tour Eiffel from almost everywhere in Paris. Nothing in Paris can compete with the Tour Eiffel.

VON BOEHM: *Whenever I see the pyramid, whatever the time of the day or in whatever season, I have a feeling that it really has the same moods as the sky of Paris, which can be very dramatic or very heavy and sometimes very gray. It really seems to be a living organism.*

PEI: I made that same argument when people questioned the pyramid. The defense of transparency was very readily accepted by the public.

A question did remain about the heat of the western sun, particularly in the summer. That problem was more difficult for me to defend against. I don't think I will ever be able to solve this problem, because I refused to put a coating on the glass. Fortunately, it only happens for a short period of time. The reflections, on the other hand, can be a plus—they change with the Parisian sky. Some people like the transparency of it but they don't like the pyramid as a shimmering object. I am not so defensive about the fact that it reflects the sky, for it is constantly changing, and that brings life to the Cour Napoléon.

VON BOEHM: *On the inside of the huge building you found more limitations—especially concerning light. How did you solve the problem of lighting the paintings? On the top floor, for example, the Salle Rubens, how did you solve this problem technically?*

PEI: I am very proud of that solution. I also know that it is not perfect. All of these galleries for paintings have to have daylight, because paintings look better under daylight, except in the winter or on a cloudy day.

Since you cannot have direct sunlight on the paintings, the conventional solution is to use diffusing glass under a skylight. Since that is no longer acceptable, the challenge was to find a way to direct unfiltered daylight to the paintings. With the help of a lighting consultant from London, Andy Sedgwick, we installed louvers to cut off direct sun rays, and large blades to direct light to the walls. With computer studies, we positioned the blades so that the light would be directed to the paintings within a certain range of angles to avoid reflection. In this regard I consider our solution a success. But the inadequacy of light in the winter is a problem. Furthermore, winter light has a bluish color which steals life from the paintings and makes the galleries gloomy and unattractive. So we have not solved all the problems.

VON BOEHM: *Paris has an especially blue light because the sky is so often gray. That gives a blue light that comes into the structure. So at some times of the year you have to have a little bit of artificial light. But they told you not to use any?*

Rendering of the interior of the German Historical Museum (by Paul Stevenson Oles)

PEI: My clients, the conservators, were purists. They liked nothing better than natural light. To convince them, I tried a piece of deception which I am not proud of. We had a full size *maquette* of a typical painting gallery built. The grilles were in place, but above the blades I had some electric lights placed, invisibly. We put a painting on the wall. The warmth of the artificial light and the winter light blended perfectly. One typically wintry day the chief conservator of paintings came and looked at the painting in the mocked-up room with the artificial light on. He walked in and looked around and up to the sky. He couldn't see the artificial light because it was hidden. He said, "Look, the painting looks fine." He would never forgive me that deception had he known.

VON BOEHM: *Then you turned the light off?*

PEI: Only after he left. And it was deadly.

VON BOEHM: *So this light has a dimmer?*

PEI: Yes, and it could not be preset, because daylight conditions vary from day to day. You really need someone with an eye to adjust it . . . that is impossible, of course.

VON BOEHM: *I know that you would like to do that personally every day!*

PEI: I go to the Louvre frequently when I am in Paris. Every time I discover something: some burnt-out lights on the pyramid, or a gallery that is improperly lighted. I still feel responsible, and I probably always will.

VON BOEHM: *In the year you finally finished the Grand Louvre project you started working on another public space: the annex to the German Historical Museum in Berlin. Why did this project seem challenging to you?*

PEI: After the Louvre, I thought no project would be too difficult. I've worked in many countries, but I had never worked in Germany before. The German Historical Museum in Berlin is my first project there. While working on the Louvre, I read a good deal on the history of France. In this case, because I do not speak or read German, I experienced unexpected difficulties. But I have been learning about Berlin, about the architecture of the city. I find this way of learning absolutely wonderful because it enriches my experience and it also enriches my architecture because I draw from the source, from the history and tradition of the place. So, if I have an opportunity to work in a country that I am not all familiar with, I welcome it, because I enjoy learning about cultures that I'm interested in.

VON BOEHM: *What have you learned about Germany?*

PEI: Not too much yet. I learned a little about the history of Germany from various friends, including yourself. In the beginning I had a naive notion that Germany was created by Bismarck after the Franco-Prussian War. That was the limit of my knowledge of German history—beyond that I knew something of Martin Luther and the Reformation. Architecturally speaking, I was less naive about what Germany had to offer. I knew something about the Baroque architecture of Germany, but my knowledge was limited. I studied under Walter Gropius and I know a lot about Bauhaus and the artists and architects who were involved with it. Before that, I had already learned to admire the neo-classical masterpieces of Schinkel.

VON BOEHM: *Why? Because of the way he uses geometry and symmetry?*

PEI: Yes, his unerring sense of proportion, which in my opinion demonstrates his mastery of geometry. The Neue Wache in Berlin is a great example. Look at the Altes Museum and King Frederick William III's villa at Charlottenburg. One is a villa, the other a monument, and both were designed with great refinement and appropriate scale. All you have to do is look at his work alongside with contemporary German architecture and there is no comparison. He stands out like Frank Lloyd Wright does in his time. So the Berlin project allowed me to learn more about Schinkel.

VON BOEHM: *The site where the annex to the German Historical Museum will be is "Schinkel country," in a way—Unter den Linden, which is very close to the Neue Wache, for instance. But first of all, it is a difficult site, I think.*

PEI: All sites are difficult, but they are difficult for different reasons. The site for the annex to the Museum is a small site, but it is in a very important part of Berlin. To me it is the cultural heart of Berlin. It's only about a five-minute walk to the Pergamon museum. You can see the site from Unter den Linden, but only barely. You know . . . the question is, what kind of building would be appropriate here? Should it be as discreet as the site, or should it compensate for it? I decided in favor of creating a presence here to attract visitors, especially since it is between two Schinkel buildings. This is the way that people would walk from Unter den Linden, past the Neue Wache, across the Spree canal, to Museum Island. So maybe we have a responsibility to say, "We are here." And that is what I did. I didn't shout with my architecture, but at the same time I wanted it to say something. After it is built I think people will say, "Yes, I see something there. Let's try and find out what it is." If it is successful in that, I will be very pleased.

VON BOEHM: *If it says, "I am here," then it is an invitation as well. Therefore it has to be something very open, which also opens up a lot of possibilities for city life to develop there, finally. I find that part of Berlin quite gray and lifeless.*

PEI: Oh yes. I had exactly that experience of grayness when I walked around to get a feeling for the site and its surrounding area. I remember in the winter of 1995 I came out of the concert hall across the Unter den Linden from the Zeughaus. The area was dark and lifeless. I decided then that this new building should be transparent and bright both day and night.

VON BOEHM: *To really bring life back to those places whose atmosphere was destroyed first by Fascism and then by Communism will take a generation or more. But you think you can help to accelerate this process with your building?*

PEI: Yes, this is exactly what I am trying to do. To make an area inviting, you have to make it transparent. This museum is a place to contain objects that you don't want to expose to daylight. So how can you justify transparency when the museum spaces themselves need to be enclosed? That was the problem. I did have to sort of stretch my program a bit to create more public space. I wanted more public space because I want people to come, and I want them to stay. If you want people to come and stay, you have to have space for them, and exciting sorts of movement within that space.

Because of the small site, we have four levels of exhibition spaces. We have designed different ways of getting from one level to another. This variety of movement systems is calculated to attract visitors to all four levels of exhibition spaces. The last and in this case the fourth level is the most difficult one to attract visitors to. I positioned the spiral stair here to offer the public a total change of pace. This leisurely ascent gives the visitors an opportunity to look out onto one of the most attractive public spaces in this part of Berlin.

VON BOEHM: *Transparency and bridges are two very important symbols. Could it be that these two things are symbols with which you want to say, "Let's build bridges. Let's make German history transparent?"*

PEI: I don't hesitate to admit that there may be this kind of symbolism; however, it is rather unconscious on my part —but I think it is nice if it is there. It needs to be transparent because we need to celebrate activity—movement. It would be a pity to put all that activity behind a wall. We already put all of our exhibits behind walls. I have no doubt that the transparency will make people notice that there is something interesting happening here. Another thing I proposed is to connect the Zeughaus to the New Wing—I call it a "new wing" but it is actually a new building connected by an underground passage to the Zeughaus. The Zeughaus is very opaque in many ways, except for its inner courtyard. I would like to bring life to that courtyard. I would like very much for the passage between the Zeughaus courtyard and the New Wing, a sort of connecting link, to bring life, to connect the present to the past. So the question was, how can we bring life to the Zeughaus? For that, I would need help from the administration and from the people in charge of monuments. They, on the other hand, have a need and a wish to keep it just the way it was. I would like to see it change, to bring this courtyard to life.

VON BOEHM: *You have brought many courtyards to life, even former parking lots, like at the Louvre.*

PEI: But it is even more needed here. If the courtyard comes alive, the Zeughaus will come alive. I would like to see a small café there. I would like to attract students from the university nearby to come, and there would be music for them, and maybe at night there would be music for people who go to concerts, to the opera. That is the kind of place that I foresee the courtyard becoming.

VON BOEHM: *Many people who know about this project also really feel that it is important because it could be a link between Eastern and Western Europe, a place of a common consciousness of history, common discussion, but also—to be more modest—a place particularly for the younger generations who have grown up in Germany after the reunification. Is all that in your mind as well?*

PEI: I can't possibly presume that . . . If it happens to serve that purpose, I would be happy and feel privileged to have done that.

VON BOEHM: *How did the Zeughaus project come about for you?*

PEI: It was—not unlike Mitterrand and the Louvre—a direct commission from Helmut Kohl, then the Chancellor of Germany. His friend and counselor, Professor Christoph Stölzl, invited me in the name of the Chancellor to consider this commission. They knew of course that I don't participate in competitions anymore. The fact that Kohl selected me directly created a debate in Germany, but it didn't last very long, and my commission was accepted. I remember when I first met with Kohl we had difficulty communicating with each other. He broke the ice, so to speak, by playing Mozart. It turned out to be a common language for the two of us. He seemed to me to possess a deep understanding of German history and hence the need to revitalize the Zeughaus.

VON BOEHM: *I see the Zeughaus annex with the great exhibition space as a bridge between the historic developments of the last 50 years in the East and West. But the building is also a bridge between different places and symbols in that very area of Berlin. It is connecting the Zeughaus with Schinkel's Neue Wache and with Unter den Linden, the main Boulevard in the center of Berlin. For me it is clearly a symbol of a new time—something like that hasn't existed there up to now.*

In your architecture, museums always seem to have the important function of connecting things: At the Miho you connected nature and art in a perfect way, and the Louvre is now a connection between the banks of the Seine. And with the museum project in Luxembourg you are again connecting two parts of the city.

PEI: When I first started to take interest in that project for an art museum in Luxembourg, I wanted to build in the city itself, on the Place du St. Esprit. The advantage seemed to be that it was within walking distance for almost all visitors. But there were too many constraints, the site was too tight. Then I was shown another site—completely different—on the opposite side of the valley that is separating Luxembourg: An old fortress called "The Three Glands." Very few people visited it and I thought: "It would be an enormous challenge to bring life to these ruins." Then I studied further and understood that right behind the fortress, at the Kirchberg, the city was expanding: a whole new development had taken place in recent years. And then I recognized that "The Three

Glands" was a place where a museum could bring the two parts of the city together because the site is right in the middle. So I recommended it to the Prime Minister.

VON BOEHM: *Your ambition is to create a visual bridge.*

PEI: Yes, you can see "The Three Glands" from the city and you will see the museum. The dialogue will be between the city and the museum's glass hall which will be illuminated at night—you will see a light on the hill. That will attract people. And they will also be attracted during the day. They will visit the hill "on the other side" and they will see the historic monument and modern art at the same time. I liked the idea of transforming a building that was once designed for wars into a place where people could enjoy the fruits of peace. That was an interesting challenge for me: How to build something new on the foundation of the fortress which is still there and may not be destroyed. How can you preserve the monument and at the same time build a museum on it? So the form of the museum has to take on the period of the fortress itself. That's why when you look at the form, it looks like the tip of an arrow. A fortress is very directional towards the anticipated enemy. So the form of the building reflects the fact that the site was a fortress once upon a time.

And then of course came all the technical requirements: Rooms were needed to house the small collection that exists already and is now expanding. Large rooms and halls were required to exhibit contemporary art which sometimes tends to produce large scale works. And a building, if it is properly done, can attract other collections as well. I hope it will do exactly that. And the exhibitions should be international. The design is flexible enough for any exhibition. And, by the way, also for other functions such as lectures or receptions for important visitors. Up to now there was no appropriate place for that in Luxembourg. The big hall where we used a lot of glass is equally attractive at daytime and nighttime and it will serve that purpose quite perfectly. After all, I can say that I am really satisfied with the Luxembourg project.

Shinji Shumeikai Bell Tower, Shiga, Japan

Miho Museum

VON BOEHM: *In Japan you designed a museum which is different from all your other projects of that kind, but also demonstrates the vast experience with public spaces you have collected over the years: the Miho Museum in the Shigaraki mountains close to Kyoto. The mountain where the building now sits was there since the beginning of time, but when you built the museum it suddenly disappeared for about two years. Can you tell that amazing story?*

PEI: I had worked for this client, a spiritual community, before. I had designed a bell tower for their sanctuary in 1988. That was about the time when I decided that I would no longer take on large projects, only some selected smaller ones.

VON BOEHM: *And then the idea came up to build a museum on a mountain ridge above a beautiful valley—a difficult site for someone like you, who are so conscious of nature, to think of building on.*

PEI: Fortunately, the restrictions of the Nature Conservancy people were working for us. They permitted us to expose only a certain amount of the building to the sky. They restricted us on height. All these restrictions were good and they worked to our advantage. We had to live within them, and as a consequence I think the building is in harmony with this particular site.

VON BOEHM: *And that is why when the building was built, the mountain was suddenly not there. Could you explain the process by which you harmonized building and nature?*

PEI: We knew from the very beginning that a good part of the building would have to be underground. The question was, how do you build a largely underground structure that is limited in area and constrained by topography? There are two ways. One is to dig into the earth and build into it, which is a very expensive and slow method, especially given the seismic problems that we had to face. So therefore the decision was made, I think largely by the builder, that it was easier to remove the earth, build the building, and then put the earth back. So the first thing they had to do was to get permission from the prefecture. The prefecture said, "Yes, you can do that, provided you put the same kind of trees back." This is exactly what we did. As a consequence, the building blends with nature much more effectively.

VON BOEHM: *Is it true that architecture has much more in common with nature than we usually think?*

PEI: Actually, you cannot separate the two from each other. I can't say that for Rome, for instance, or for Paris, because they are largely manmade artifacts. Even the River Seine in Paris is a manmade object. Nature's water is running through it, but man channeled it in an architectural way. Look at the works of Le Nôtre, the great seventeenth-century French landscape architect. He reshaped nature into a work of architecture. I can think of no better example to illustrate the difference between the East and the West with respect to the relationship between architecture and nature. When I was working on the Miho Museum in Japan, I was very much concerned with that relationship. I find that challenge a very welcome one.

VON BOEHM: *In the entrance hall to the museum, we get a feeling of a temple. And the approach to the building is like coming to a sacred place. Can you explain the elements you included in this particular space, and why?*

PEI: The approach to the museum was a matter of paramount importance. My client took great pains to find this site, which is located in a large nature preserve. It is considered to be a sacred place, once chosen to be the site for an important temple. This obliged us to take great care in placing the museum with minimum disturbance of the surrounding nature. My client and I both felt it was inappropriate for visitors to drive to the entrance in a car, for example.

VON BOEHM: *In addition to considering nature, you responded to culture. Even in the glass construction, especially in the roof, we find elements that remind us of old Japanese traditions. The silhouette of the building is very important. To me it is quite obvious that you must have studied Japanese structures such as Katsura intensively.*

PEI: In this case, I drew my inspiration from the large farmhouses of the Edo period.

VON BOEHM: *You also used the tetrahedron—the entire roof structure is elaborated on this geometric form. Why does it match the landscape so ideally?*

PEI: Because it produces peaks and valleys. The piling up of tetrahedron structures in steel creates great structural rigidity and spatial complexity, much like the large wooden beam construction of the Edo farmhouses. As we were obliged to expose only a fraction of the building to the sky, I decided to cover it with glass. So sunshading was necessary, and we chose aluminum that looks like wood. These "wooden" sunscreens bring a lot of filtered warm light into the building. But these details are of secondary importance.

The first challenge, as I said earlier, was how to develop harmony between nature and the building. The second one I think is a question of melding tradition with modernity. This is a building built in our times . . . but I had the responsibility to respect the tradition that has developed through the centuries. In fact, those two challenges are related.

VON BOEHM: *And in view of those challenges, immediately the question arises: what should a modern building in Japan be like? How did you approach this question?*

PEI: It would be presumptuous for a foreign architect to suggest what a modern building in Japan should be like. I'm quite familiar with the works of contemporary Japanese architects. They are the ones qualified to answer this question. My personal view is that it would have to be rooted in their own cultural history. Like a tree, it has to be rooted in its soil. Cross-pollination will happen with time, only when it is accepted in its native environment.

VON BOEHM: *To get to the site where you built the museum you had to pass a narrow valley. You had to climb, and you even needed special devices to climb. How did you solve the problem of access?*

PEI: The site is like a peninsula surrounded by nature untouched by man. It is a ridge—a very high ridge—which drops rather precipitously on three sides down to the road. So there is no way to get up there without damaging nature. So it was good luck that our client owned a piece of land on the other side of this hill to the east, which they used for parking. So I thought, instead of winding our way up from the road, destroying nature in the process, why don't we dig a tunnel from the other side, build a bridge over the valley, and approach the building from the bridge?

I remembered a story written by a famous fourth-century Chinese philosopher poet, Tao Yuanming. A fisherman rowed a boat down a stream, as he had been doing for years. But for some reason, this time he saw something different. He saw a grove of peach trees with beautiful flowers and white petals on the ground, and said, "I don't remember this." So he abandoned his boat and walked through the peach grove. As he got closer to the source of the stream, he saw a little opening in the mountain. He walked into the opening and through a narrow passage. After many steps, the path opened up to reveal a neatly cultivated expanse inhabited by a community of people of unfamiliar dress and speech. He learned that they were the descendants of a clan that had escaped the turmoil of war by settling there hundreds of years ago.

That story gave me the idea to propose a tunnel and a bridge. Fortunately, both Mrs. and Ms. Koyama had read that essay by Tao Yuanming and liked the sense of detachment this approach would give to the museum. This joint sharing of an idea enabled us to overcome the many difficulties. First, we had to buy the hill over the tunnel from a demanding seller. Then we had to persuade both the prefecture and the national government, which both have jurisdiction over the nature preserve, to allow the bridge. Were it not for the strong commitment on the part of the client we would still be trying to find a way to approach the museum.

VON BOEHM: *It was a small paradise on earth in the beginning, but it became a bigger and bigger project.*

PEI: Yes, I know. It started as a small museum to contain Mrs. Koyama's collection, which consists of ceremonial objects for the tea ceremony, and some Chinese paintings of high quality. Since then, the Shumei Family has expanded the collection to include a collection of art objects from the Silk Route—all the way from Japan to the Mediterranean, via China. That collection was added to during the last ten years. Therefore, while we were designing the building we had to make many changes along the way to accommodate the increasing collection. Fortunately we could dig into the earth, to build underground. There was a certain amount of improvisation. In a way, I think it turned out rather nicely, because it makes the experience of coming to this museum a much richer one due to its collection of masterpieces of art rarely found in Japan.

VON BOEHM: *Light, as always in your work, plays a very important role in this museum.*

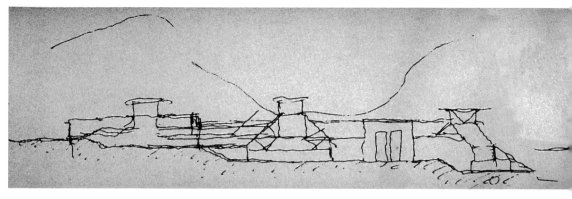

Above: I.M. Pei's study for
the Miho Museum

Below: Interior of the Miho
Museum

PEI: I think so. I consider light, daylight especially, of
fundamental importance to architecture. There is no space
without light; there is no form without light. It is not an ex-
aggeration to say that light is the key to architecture.

VON BOEHM: *We can feel this at the Miho Museum almost
physically, when light hits the marble walls and floors through
the glass roof. Can you explain the construction of the roof?*

PEI: When you look up you might think that this is a
very complex structure. In fact it is not. There is a system to
this construction, and the system is based on the triangle. I
believe in the triangle because it is the simplest and strongest geometric construct. Yet one can create great spatial
complexity through juxtaposition and combination. It is a

lot like the music of Bach, which you know well. The music of Bach is a variation on a theme, and yet what richness he was able to give it! It continues to impress me and influence my architecture. I like simplicity, but at the same time I don't like monotony. So therefore the question arises, how can you reconcile the two?

VON BOEHM: *Light also interacts with the system of construction you designed. The shadows seem to form a kind of forest of bamboo.*

PEI: The shadows are formed by the sunshades under the glass roof. In the beginning the shadows bothered me. But now I no longer worry about it, because the shadow patterns change all the time. In fact, I find the constantly changing pattern quite fascinating.

VON BOEHM: *Also, the stone you used gives a special light. It brings out the beauty of the stone, a sense of permanence, and a history that goes back millions and millions of years.*

PEI: I like the warm color of the Magny stone. I have specified it in many of my projects. Furthermore, since it is a natural product, each piece is different. In a wall, this produces a richness like a piece of tapestry.

VON BOEHM: *In a rather quiet, remote area of the Miho Museum, you created an atrium garden with holy stones, which play a very important role in Japanese culture.*

PEI: At the very beginning of this project, the museum was intended to house a collection of mostly Japanese art, for the tea ceremony. This part of the collection is housed in today's North Wing. It was designed with a stone garden in the middle. It is traditional and not original. What was interesting was the agreement by the client to expand the collection beyond Japanese art. Since there are many similar collections in Japan, I wondered why people would want to come so far to see something they could see in Tokyo or Osaka. I raised this question. The Koyamas obviously thought of this as well. The question was, what should be collected to compliment their present collection? I suggested that perhaps they should consider the other influences on Japanese art beyond China and Korea. But what were those influences? I suggested they look west beyond China, to follow the paths that spread religion and trade to Japan. And indeed that was the decision they made. They then found a Japanese art dealer who proved to be knowledgeable and well connected in this field. It was Mr. Noriyoshi Horiuchi who helped the Koyamas to create their other collection, which is housed in the South Wing of the Museum.

VON BOEHM: *And you expanded the museum to incorporate that collection?*

PEI: We extended it step by step as they made the new collection. When they made a new acquisition, we had to find a place for it. Due to the strict limits imposed by the nature preserve regulations, we had to expand largely underground.

VON BOEHM: *And yet still you have—for certain objects—enough light coming from the roofs?*

PEI: Fortunately most of the objects are better displayed under artificial light. For certain three-dimensional objects, stone sculptures for example, we had to design inconspicuous light shafts to direct daylight to the objects.

VON BOEHM: *And there was a special requirement for some of the rooms: Shinji Shumeikai asked you to create a visual connection with their sanctuary on a mountaintop on the other side of the valley, and also with the bell tower you had designed for them some years before.*

PEI: That indeed created a difficulty, because the rooms from which you could see the sanctuary needed a big window. But this would allow too much light to shine in on the exposed art objects. And it would create reflections on the display cases. It produced problems for us and for the curators.

VON BOEHM: *It is the same in filmmaking. You can never combine bright outside light with the inside of a room with relatively dim light in one shot—in a pan, for instance. But that's what people do at a museum when they look out and then "pan" back to the room with their eyes.*

PEI: So what do you do in film?

VON BOEHM: *We cover the window with a special foil that partly takes the light away to prevent the image from being overexposed, but still allows one to see everything outside—it makes a very natural impression.*

PEI: That is exactly what we did—we placed two layers of woven fabric shades inside the glass opening, which enable the curators to control the amount of daylight entering the room. You can see the sanctuary and the bell tower on the other side of the valley in a quite magical way.

VON BOEHM: *In history, the Chinese and Japanese have not always been friends. Was it difficult, or is it difficult now, to work in Japan? What was your experience? What did you learn?*

PEI: I learned one lesson over those ten delightful years: politics is one thing, but when it comes to people, it is vastly different. People dealt with me not as a Chinese or Japanese but as an architect—I am an architect, and I have my ideas and they are what they are—we dealt with each other on human terms. In the beginning there was a barrier because of language. But I feel there was less of a barrier for me with my Chinese background because we shared the same cultural tradition.

Back to the Future:
Bank of China, Hong Kong

VON BOEHM: *How did the Bank of China building in Hong Kong come about?*

PEI: In 1982, two representatives of the bank came to see my father, because he was once general manager of the bank. (That was before the government took over the bank.) These two representatives—one of the two was chairman of the board, I believe—asked my father for permission to persuade me to design this building. It was a very Chinese kind of gesture of respect. My father was very ill at that time, but they invited him to come back and be one of the permanent directors. My father said, "Thank you very much. If you had asked me a few years ago, I probably would have said yes, but not now." He died shortly afterward. He said that designing their building was my decision, and they should ask me. That's what they did, and I accepted. Incidentally, my father initiated the construction of the old Bank of China building in Hong Kong in the twenties. He was the manager at that time.

VON BOEHM: *You were confronted with much Chinese mythology when you designed this building. When you first started to design, you compared it to a bamboo which grows.*

PEI: The problem I faced in Hong Kong was "feng shui," which literally means "wind and water." It has its roots in the worship of the forces of nature, which sometimes degenerated into a form of superstition. When you design buildings in Hong Kong, you cannot get away from that problem. There are specialists, feng shui masters, who advise people on all matter of things, especially on the selection of a building site; placement of the building on the site; and the shape and form of the building. I was aware of this, but did not take it seriously. As soon as we made our design public, I was immediately attacked—just as fiercely as I was attacked for the Louvre, but for entirely different reasons. For instance, they attacked our building because it had too many sharp corners. They said, "The corners are like the blades of a sword, which will bring bad luck to one's neighbors." There were many other objections. Fortunately, my client supported me to the end.

VON BOEHM: *Looking back, how would you describe the challenge?*

PEI: Remember that I undertook the project in 1982. By 1997, Hong Kong would be returned to China by Great Britain. I sensed from the beginning that my clients, the representatives of the Bank in Hong Kong, were aware of the symbolic importance of this project. The challenge for me, frankly speaking, was architectural. Only a few years before, our neighbor, the Hong Kong & Shanghai Bank, had just completed its new headquarters designed by Norman Foster, to wide acclaim. I admit with some embarrassment today that I felt compelled to respond even with limited means and on a less than ideal site.

VON BOEHM: *It was an incredibly small and difficult site.*

PEI: The site was surrounded by a heavily trafficked roadway that they called a roundabout. There was no possibility to make an entrance. I had to find a way to gain access to the site. I proposed to create a new road at the back of our site: we obtained planning department approval after a long and difficult negotiation. That was the first thing I did.

In spite of its many shortcomings, the site had one important advantage. Because it was located just out of the airport flight path, the new building was not restricted by the height limit imposed on all buildings to the north. A tall building would permit us to overlook some of the most prestigious buildings of Hong Kong, with a panoramic view of the harbor and Kowloon beyond. The next challenge was what kind of tall building, and how to make it structurally expressive.

VON BOEHM: *Talking about structure—there are also requirements to give a certain structure to a tall building like that because of the forces of nature alone.*

PEI: To design a skyscraper, the designer has to reckon with a wind force in Hong Kong approximately twice that for the City of New York, and three times that of Los Angeles.

VON BOEHM: . . . *which means that the structure becomes very important. It has to be rigid but it cannot be too rigid. Rigidity is also a problem because an overly rigid structure will break. That is why bamboo is a very good example. Did you consider the principle of bamboo when you were thinking about this seventy-story building?*

PEI: Indeed, I was thinking about bamboo metaphorically.

I.M. Pei demonstrating how the Bank of China, Hong Kong, is joined together in three dimensions

But my engineer, Leslie Robertson, was not thinking about bamboo. He was thinking about something else. He said that the entire building should be joined together in three dimensions. Almost all vertical loads would be transferred to the four corner columns at the base of the building. I don't know if you know that a huge structural member goes through the heart of the building. Most people don't know that. This engineering tour de force enabled us to reduce the total tonnage of steel to only half that used in the lightest of comparable buildings in Hong Kong.

VON BOEHM: *But in your building the whole structure is also a kind of refinement, and that alone must have been quite satisfying. Do you regret not having done more tall buildings of such significance?*

PEI: I have designed tall buildings previously in the United States and Canada. The Bank of China in Hong Kong presented us with a challenge to find a structural solution that could resist the powerful forces of nature in the most effective way.

Do I regret not having done more tall buildings of significance? My answer is both yes and no. In recent years I have tended to prefer smaller projects so that I can concentrate my attention on refining my design. On the other hand, I have discovered new formal possibilities in tall buildings that continue to tempt me. About seven years ago I assisted my two architect sons (Pei Partnership Architects) in a similarly large project in Jakarta. Unfortunately, it was aborted during the early stages of construction due to the political upheaval in Indonesia.

VON BOEHM: *Is the triangle your favorite geometric form?*

PEI: I don't have any favorite geometric form . . . I like the triangle for its rigidity in the structural sense. I explored curvilinear surfaces in the Meyerson Symphony Hall in Dallas, for instance, for spatial rather than for structural reasons. In the sixties I visited many Baroque churches in Austria and Germany. I was fascinated by the effect of curvilinear surfaces on space. They undulate seductively when one moves through them. However, I failed to experiment with it in my buildings partly due to the constraint of materials such as stone, glass, or steel. Those Baroque churches used stucco. Le Corbusier's Ronchamp Chapel was built with gunite; those were plastic materials. Today's computers do enable us to design and build complex spaces and forms. Yet the constraint of materials remains a challenge.

VON BOEHM: *Is it important to you that people who enter a building that you have designed can feel it physically, with all their senses?*

PEI: That is what every architect attempts to do with greater or lesser success. Frank Lloyd Wright is a master in this; his buildings invariably oblige one to enter a low space and then they explode into a high space. This simple device never fails to engage a visitor with an element of surprise.

VON BOEHM: *As does the East Wing of the National Gallery.*

PEI: I did use the same device at the East Wing of the National Gallery of Art in Washington. To that I added another element of surprise for the visitor, the spatial excitement created by the triangular module. Most buildings are designed with a parallel grid which has two vanishing points. The triangular grid has three vanishing points. As one moves through such a space, the additional vanishing point adds complexity to one's perception of space.

VON BOEHM: *What is the limit for you? When does one have to stop playing with structures, playing with geometry? There is a certain limit in your architecture.*

PEI: Structure is always a factor in architecture, but it becomes more important when you have special situations, such as an extremely tall building or one where there is a natural phenomenon such as extremely strong wind and/or seismic movement. I would say that the play of forms and spaces should be the major preoccupation for architects. Now, when you talk about form and space, you have to take into consideration light and the movement of people, which animate both form and space to create architecture. When you take them all together, you can have a wonderful time with architecture.

VON BOEHM: *Why was movement always so enormously important for you? I know many architects and I've talked to them about architecture, but movement is not really a subject for many of them. How did it come to be so for you?*

PEI: From, I think, observation. I like to think that buildings are designed for people. For that reason, I prefer to design public buildings, which usually are used by a lot of people who will interact with that spatial experience, and hopefully will be affected by it. Not all buildings are equally effective in that sense. Office buildings, for instance—which I don't find too interesting for that reason. I think that is the exciting thing about designing buildings that maximize the opportunity to see people moving in a space.

Bank of China Building, Beijing

VON BOEHM: *Some years ago you decided not to take commissions for very tall buildings any more, but to take small projects instead.*

PEI: Because this kind of work gives me greater freedom to design and less involvement in day-to-day management.

VON BOEHM: *But then suddenly you broke the promise you had made to yourself. You accepted a commission to design the biggest bank building in the world—the Bank of China in Beijing.*

PEI: I was reluctant to accept that commission at first. I dreaded the thought of making frequent trips to Beijing. When the Bank suggested appointing Pei Partnership Architects, my sons' firm, to be the principal in charge, I accepted to act as design consultant for the project.

It is a huge building, with almost 200,000 square meters of space. As the site is located only one mile (approximately) from the Forbidden City, it has a height restriction, which forced it to become an ungainly monolith of a building. The only solution we found acceptable was to carve out a large void in the middle to make a garden so that there would be light and a view for the interior offices.

VON BOEHM: *So actually it is a kind of atrium system with glass roofs.*

PEI: That is an obvious solution, but the challenge was "what kind of garden?" As the scale of the void is

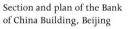
Section and plan of the Bank of China Building, Beijing

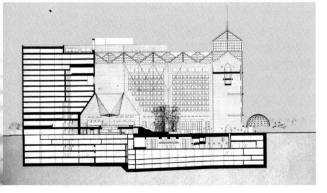
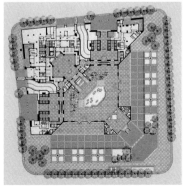

enormous—55 meters square—and to protect it from the well-known "Peking dust," it had to be glazed to become an atrium. That made the garden solution even more difficult. We decided to combat the scale problem in four ways.

Since it is a garden, we introduced natural elements into it. We found 20-meter tall bamboo from Hangchow, and a group of 2- to 5-meter rocks from Kunming's stone forest, which are almost at home in such a space. Next we proposed a use for the space, i.e., public banking functions, that would bring people in to humanize the space. Thirdly, we terraced the garden to accommodate multiple levels for different kinds of public banking needs. Lastly, large glazed openings to the south and east were used to create the desired transparency, which is functionally and symbolically important. Furthermore, it visually expands the large enclosed atrium into the city of Beijing. Thus, by humanizing the space, by making it transparent, and by visually opening it to the city as a whole, we provided a symbolic opening and a bridge between present, past, and future.

VON BOEHM: *Is my assumption correct that it was not only a challenge but also an obligation to do that?*

PEI: Yes, it was an obligation, definitely. Definitely an obligation to China and also to my father. My father belonged to the first generation of modern bankers in China. He spent his entire career in that bank. In those days they used an abacus; now they use computers. That kind of change in less than a century is simply beyond comprehension. There is simply no way to express the continuity of tradition architecturally.

But in a way we solved it in the Beijing project. I am satisfied with the design we arrived at for the Bank of China.

Design and Style

VON BOEHM: *There are many architects like your friend Breuer and other Bauhaus people who did a lot of design and furniture. I don't think you have ever been into anything like that.*

PEI: Yes, I did at one time. During the war I started to design furniture, but only for a short time. I was working in an engineering firm designing things that were of no interest to me. So with the little time I had at lunchtime, I would design furniture. At that time I thought it would be interesting to make something out of bamboo. I had some made actually, but I never went very far with it. Furniture is very difficult to do. I learned to respect the furniture done by Le Corbusier, Breuer, Mies, and also Aalto. I would have liked to be able to say that I have designed furniture too, but that was not to be. Once I came to New York to work with Zeckendorf, I had no time, no time at all except to work with him and for him. For twelve years of my life I was totally engaged in projects of property for development. I would have liked to pursue furniture design; that would have added a great deal to my life as an architect.

VON BOEHM: *Some architects design not only furniture but also things for daily life, coffeepots and things like that. What do you think about this tendency?*

PEI: I am not envious of that. I find furniture very different from coffeepots. Furniture is a complement to architecture and coffeepots are not. So there is a difference between the two. I envy those who can design beautiful furniture, but not those who design coffeepots. Before the nineteenth century furniture was essentially made of wood, which depends on a craft tradition. Perhaps the most refined example is the furniture made in China during the Ming Dynasty, in the sixteenth century. Bent metal, laminated wood, and plastics are relatively modern inventions that contributed greatly to modern furniture design.

VON BOEHM: *Mr. Pei, do you envy those who can say that they have created a school of architecture?*

PEI: Frankly, I have never thought of that. I have been immersed in problem solving of my own. The process of analysis is a very personal one based on my own value systems formed through years of trying to understand the society in which I live and work. My approach to design is no different from that of any other architect; it is the creation of the most exciting and appropriate forms and spaces for the subject at hand. The key is the analytical process one goes through in search of truth, as I see it. I belong to no group nor do I engage myself in the architectural movements of the moment. This will not lead to the development of a particular signature style, which is necessary to attract a following, especially among young architects.

VON BOEHM: *Your approach to architecture is not really your personal style which you actually deny to have because you really deal with problems when they come . . .*

PEI: For me, each problem is a distinct challenge. The excitement of architecture is in its ever-changing possibilities of design. It is the result of a process of analysis, which is very difficult to teach. I suppose I must have a personal style, like my handwriting. But it is not consciously arrived at.

VON BOEHM: *Maybe "style" is not the appropriate word in connection with your work. But if you look closer and deeper, you will immediately see it. Your architecture is not signature architecture for the (sake of) signature. Many architects are seduced to produce buildings for their signature. They are hired—at least partly—for their signature.*

PEI: I think that is correct. I think the signature is in itself a constraint. I don't envy the architects who have such a strong stylistic stamp that clients would be disappointed if they do not get the same "look" in their projects. I don't envy them. I think I have greater freedom without that.

VON BOEHM: *No style and no signature . . . I don't know . . . your buildings do have something in common. I've looked at the photographs of Kips Bay and I immediately found similarities with the Earth Science Building at M.I.T., and there is a similarity between, let's say, the East Wing of the National Gallery of Art and the new building for the Bank of China in Beijing.*

PEI: But you will agree if I say that this is not enough to

create a real "school." the question that you have just asked is a question that I have raised constantly in my own mind. That is why there is no Pei School. For me the important distinction is between a stylistic approach to the design; and an analytical approach giving the process of due consideration to time, place, and purpose. These three essential elements are all variables. Look at NCAR at Boulder and then compare it to Kips Bay in New York. They are in two different worlds. How can you apply a signature look?

My analytical approach requires a full understanding of the three essential elements—time, place, purpose—to arrive at an ideal balance among them. Design considerations exist during the entire process. Design becomes the dominant force in the end to make the project a work of architecture.

VON BOEHM: *As in science, there are different ways to analyze . . . you have different ways to get to a result. There are different ways to get to a solution in architecture. The way that you analyze your problem is where your kind of signature starts, and at the end it is not imposing anything but still it is there in a quite discrete way. But as we talk about signature one question comes to mind: isn't it a sign of our times that we are living in a world where brands, trademarks, and names are so very important—sometimes in an almost ridiculous way?*

PEI: I think so. Maybe it is a substitute for something else people are missing. This question of yours interests me very much. I am confident that the stylistic approach to architecture is not mine. I have developed a certain analytical process and design sensibility which are peculiar to myself. I think that somehow it would indeed give my work a certain personality. That is what I hope.

VON BOEHM: *we are talking about a similarity of a kind of spirit that is not too obvious but can be felt by the visitor . . .*

PEI: Architecture is there to enhance life. It is not just an object in space to look at—it would be superficial to reduce architecture to that aspect. It has to contain human activity. It has to make that activity noble. That is the way I look at it. I hope people will identify my work with that.

VON BOEHM: *Where will it go? What is, for you, the future of architecture?*

PEI: One important direction architecture is taking now has to do with the digital age. The computer has already given us possibilities that we never had before. In that sense it has tremendous possibilities. I have not begun to be involved in it, but it is very important for the future generation of architects.

It makes it possible for us to create and build the most complex forms and spaces but it also has its limits. It cannot plumb the depth of time nor can it refine our design sensibilities. Innovative technology provides us with new tools—it is what we do with them that matters. Architecture, like all cultural artifacts has its roots in history. The French have a wise saying, "Plus ça change, plus c'est la même chose." As I have said before, the variables of time, place, and purpose inherent in each project will continue to challenge architects with limitless permutations and combinations to create. As we enter into a time of rapid change, I am more optimistic than ever about the future of architecture.

Biographical Notes on I. M. Pei

Born April 26, 1917 in
Canton, China
Naturalized citizen of the United States

EDUCATION

Massachusetts Institute of Technology
B. Arch. 1940
Harvard Graduate School of Design
M. Arch. 1946
Massachusetts Institute of Technology
Alpha Rho Chi Medal 1940
Massachusetts Institute of Technology
Traveling Fellowship 1940
Massachusetts Institute of Technology
AIA Medal 1940
Harvard Graduate School of Design
Wheelwright Traveling Fellowship 1951
Doctor of Fine Arts Honorary Degree
Harvard University/New York University/University of Pennsylvania/
Rensselaer Polytechnic Institute/Carnegie-Mellon University/
Northeastern University/University of Massachusetts/University of
Rochester/Brown University/Dartmouth College
Doctor of Laws Honorary Degree
Chinese University of Hong Kong/Pace University
Doctor of Humane Letters Honorary Degree
Columbia University/University of Colorado/University of Hong Kong/
American University of Paris

ASSOCIATION MEMBERSHIPS

American Institute of Architects
Fellow, elected 1964
Royal Institute of British Architects
American Society of Interior Designers
Honorary Fellow, elected 1970
American Academy & Institute of Arts & Letters
Elected to Academy 1975, elected to Institute 1963 (Chancellorship 1978–80)
American Academy of Arts and Sciences
Elected 1967
National Academy of Design
Academician, elected 1965
Urban Design Council of the City of New York
1967–72
AIA National Urban Policy Task Force
1970–74
National Council on the Humanities, *1966–70*
AIA Task Force on the West Front of the U.S. Capitol
1978–80
The Corporation of the Massachusetts Institute of Technology
1972–77   1978–83
National Council on the Arts
1981–84
Institut de France
Foreign Associate, elected 1983
New York City Partnership, Inc.
Board of Directors, elected 1986
Museum of Fine Arts, Boston
Board of Overseers, Honorary Member, elected 1986

Royal Academy of Arts, London
  Honorary Academician, elected 1993
Chinese Academy of Engineering
  Foreign Member, elected June 1996
Membre de l'Académie d'Architecture de France
  1997

Pei Cobb Freed & Partners/I.M. Pei & Partners, New York
  Founding Partner, 1955–
Webb & Knapp, Inc.
  Director of Architecture, 1948–55
Harvard Graduate School of Design
  Assistant Professor, 1945–48
National Defense Research Committee
  1943–45

AWARDS

National Institute of Arts and Letters -
  Arnold Brunner Award, 1961
New York Chapter of the American Institute of Architects -
  Medal of Honor, 1963
International Institute of Boston - *Golden Door Award, 1970*
The City Club of New York - *For New York Award, 1973*
The Thomas Jefferson Memorial Medal for Architecture, *1976*
American Society of Interior Designers -
  Elsie de Wolfe Award, 1978
Rhode Island School of Design - *President's Fellow, 1979*
American Academy of Arts & Letters -
  Gold Medal for Architecture, 1979
The American Institute of Architects - *The Gold Medal, 1979*
National Arts Club - *Gold Medal of Honor, 1981*
City of New York -
  Mayor's Award of Honor for Art and Culture, 1981
Académie d'Architecture (France) -
  La Grande Médaille d'Or, 1981
The Pritzker Architecture Prize, 1983
Académie des Beaux-Arts -
  Associé Etranger, Institut de France, 1984
The Medal of Liberty, 1986
National Medal of Art, 1988
Praemium Imperiale for lifetime achievement
  in architecture (Japan), *1989*
University of California at Los Angeles -
  UCLA Gold Medal, 1990
Colbert Foundation -
  First Award for Excellence, 1991
Excellence 2000 Award, 1991
Medal of Freedom, 1993
Officier de La Légion d'Honneur (France), *1993*
New York State Governor's Arts Award, 1994
National Endowment for the Arts -
  Medal of Arts/Ambassador for the Arts Award, 1994
Architectural Society of China (Beijing)
  Gold Medal for Outstanding Achievement in Architecture, 1994
The Bezalel Academy of Arts & Design of Jerusalem -
  Jerusalem Prize for Arts & Letters, 1994
Municipal Arts Society, New York City -
  Jacqueline Kennedy Onassis Medal, February, 1996
Premio Internazionale Novecento La Rosa D'Oro, 1996
Brown University
  Independent Award, 1997
The MacDowell Colony
  Edward MacDowell Medal, 1998
B2 Kulturpreis (Germany), 1999
Historic Landmark Preservation Center, New York
  Cultural Laureate, 1999

Catalog of Works

I.M.Pei is the design principal of the following projects:

U.S. National Bank of
Denver/Mile High Center
Denver, Colorado
1952–1956

*Washington Square East/
Society Hill*
Philadelphia, Pennsylvania
1957–1964

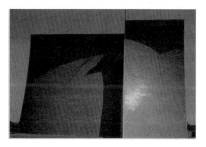

The Luce Chapel
Taichung, Taiwan, 1954–1963

*Green Center for the Earth
Sciences*
Massachusetts Institute of
Technology
Cambridge, Massachusetts
1959–1964

Kips Bay Plaza
New York, NY, 1957–1962

National Airlines Terminal (now TWA Domestic Terminal)
Kennedy International Airport, New York, NY, 1960–1970

Everson Museum of Art
Syracuse, NY, 1961–1964

Air Traffic Control Towers
Federal Aviation Agency
Various airports, USA
1962–1967 through 1970

School of Journalism/Newhouse Communica-
tions Center, Syracuse University
Syracuse, NY, 1961–1964

New College
Sarasota, Florida, 1963–1967

University Plaza/New
York University
New York, NY 1961–1966

The Wilmington Tower
Wilmington, Delaware,
1963–1971

National Center for
Atmospheric Research
Boulder, Colorado
1961–1967

Camille Edouard Dreyfus Chemistry Building
Massachusetts Institute of Technology, Cambridge,
Massachusetts, 1964–1970

The John Fitzgerald Kennedy Library
Boston, Massachusetts, 1965–1979
Theodore J. Musho, Associate Partner-in-Charge

Dallas City Hall
Dallas, Texas, 1966–1977,
Theodore J. Musho, Associate Partner-in-Charge

Des Moines Art Center Addition
Des Moines, Iowa, 1966–1968

*Canadian Imperial Bank
of Commerce*
Toronto, Canada, 1967–1973

Bedford-Stuyvesant Superblock
Brooklyn, NY, 1966–1969

Paul Mellon Center for the Arts
The Choate School, Wallingford, Connecticut, 1968–1972

Cleo Rogers Memorial Library
Columbus, Indiana, 1966–1971

Herbert F. Johnson Museum of Art
Cornell University, Ithaca, NY, 1968–1973

National Gallery of Art/East Building
Washington, D.C., 1968–1978
Leonard Jacobson, Partner-in-Charge of Project Management

Museum of Fine Arts/West Wing
Boston, Massachusetts, 1977–1981

Oversea-Chinese Banking Corporation Centre
Singapore, 1970–1976

IBM Office Building
Purchase, New York, 1977–1984

Laura Spellman Rockefeller Hall
Princeton University,
Princeton, New Jersey
1973

Texas Commerce Tower/ United Energy Plaza
Houston, Texas, 1978–1982
Harold Fredenburgh, Associa
Partner-in-Charge

Raffles City
Singapore, 1973–1986

The Wiesner Building
Massachusetts Institute of Technology
Cambridge, Massachusetts, 1978–1984

Fragrant Hill Hotel
Beijing, China
1979–1982

The Gateway
Singapore
1981–1991

The Jacob K. Javits Center of New York
New York, NY, 1979–1986, James Ingo Freed
Partner-in-Charge of Design, Werner Wandelmaier
Partner-in-Charge of Project Management

Bank of China Tower
Hong Kong, 1982–1989

*Miami World Trade Center
(CenTrust Tower)*
Miami, Florida
1980–1987

The Morton H. Meyerson Symphony Center
Dallas, Texas, 1982–1989

*The Mt. Sinai Medical
Center Modernization*
New York, New York
Phase I: 1981–1989;
Phase II: 1989–1992

Grand Louvre
Paris, France, Phase I – Cour Napoleon 1983–1989
Leonard Jacobson, Partner-in-Charge of Project Management

Choate Rosemary Hall Science Center
Wallingford, Connecticut, 1986–1989

Four Seasons Hotel
New York, New York
1989–1993

*Creative Artists
Agency Headquarters*
Beverly Hills, California,
1986–1989

Grand Louvre
Paris, France, Phase II – Richelieu Wing,
Carrousel, Pyramide Inversée, 1990–1993

Rock and Roll Hall of Fame and Museum
Cleveland, Ohio, 1987–1995

Miho Museum
Shiga, Japan, 1991–1997

*Shinji Shumeikai Bell
Tower*
Shiga, Japan
1988–1990

*Basil & Elise Goulandris
Museum of Modern Art*
Athens, Greece
In design

Musée d'Art Moderne Grand-Duc Jean
Luxembourg, Under construction

German Historical Museum
Berlin, Under construction

Urban planning projects:

Southwest Washington Redevelopment
Washington, D.C.
1953–1968

Government Center Plan/ City of Boston
Boston, Massachusetts
1960–1961
Henry N. Cobb, Partner-Collaborator

Central Business District Plan
Oklahoma City, Oklahoma
1963–1964

Master Plan/Columbia University
New York, NY
1968–1970
Henry N. Cobb, Partner-Collaborator

Selected Bibliography

Betsky, Aaron. *Architecture & Medicine: I.M. Pei Designs the Kirklin Clinic*. University of Alabama Health Services Foundation at the University of Alabama at Birmingham Medical Center. Lanham: University Press of America, 1992.

Cannell, Michael T. *I.M. Pei: Mandarin of Modernism*. New York: Carol Southern Books, 1995.

Casper, Dale E. *Ieoh Ming Pei, Architect: Journal Literature in Review*. Monticello, IL: Vance Bibliographies, 1988.

Chaine, Catherine. *Le Grand Louvre*. Paris: Hatier, 1989.

Davis, William, and Christina Tree. *The Kennedy Library*. Exton, PA: Schiffer, 1980.

Dean, Andrea. "Conversations: I.M. Pei." *AIA Journal*, June 1979.

Diamondstein, Barbaralee. *American Architecture Now*. New York: Rizzoli, 1980.

Filler, Martin. "P/A on Pei: Roundtable on a Trapezoid." *Progressive Architecture*, October 1978.

First Person Singular: I.M. Pei. Peter Rosen. PBS Home Video, 1997.

Heyer, Paul. *Architects on Architecture*. New York: Walker, 1966.

I M. Pei & Partners Drawings for the East Building, National Gallery of Art, Its Evolution in Sketches, Renderings, and Models, 1968–1978 (exh. cat.). Washington, D.C.: Adams Davidson Galleries, 1978.

I.M. Pei & Partners. *National Center for Atmospheric Research, Boulder Colorado, 1967: I.M. Pei & Partners and Araldo Cossutta, Christian Science Church Center, Boston Massachusetts, 1973*. Ed. Yukio Futagawa. Tokyo: A. D. A. EDITA Tokyo, 1976.

Ieoh Ming Pei. Thomas M.C. Johnston, and François Warin. Antenne 2., Caméras Continentales, Palm Production, Télé-Europe, 1986.

Lansford, Henry. *UCAR at 25*. Boulder: University Corporation for Atmospheric Research, 1985.

Mandarin der Moderne – Der Architekt I.M. Pei. Gero von Boehm. Interscience Film. Arte, Germany. March 4, 1998 and ZDF, Germany. July 8, 1998.

The Museum on the Mountain. Peter Rosen. Shumei Culture Foundation, 1998.

Pei, Ieoh Ming. "Urban Renewal in Southwest Washington." *AIA Journal*, January 1963.

"China Won't Ever Be the Same." *New York Times*, June 22, 1989.

Prentice, Helaine Kaplan. *Suzhou: Shaping an Ancient City for the New China: A DEAW/Pei Workshop*. Washington, D.C.: Spacemaker Press, 1998.

Reid, Aileen. *I.M. Pei*. New York: Knickerbocker Press, 1995.

Schmertz, Mildred F. "Getting Ready for the John F. Kennedy Library: Not Everyone Wants To Make It Go Away." *Architectural Record*, December 1974.

Spring, Bernard. "Evaluation: From Context to Form, I.M. Pei's National Center for Atmospheric Research." *AIA Journal*, June 1979.

Suner, Bruno. *Ieoh Ming Pei*. Paris: Hazan, 1988.

Warner, Lucy. *The National Center for Atmospheric Research: An Architectural Masterpiece*. Boulder: NCAR, 1985.

Wiseman, Carter. *I.M. Pei: A Profile in American Architecture*. New York: H.N. Abrams, 1990.

Cover: Portrait of I.M. Pei
(photograph by Udo Hesse);
Grand Louvre, Phase I (photograph by
Owen Franken)

Editorial direction by Claudine Weber-Hof

Manuscript edited by Bruce Murphy
Project management in New York:
Nancy Robinson
Photo research: Victor Orlewicz, Mamaroneck,
New York

© Prestel Verlag
Munich · London · New York, 2000

Library of Congress Catalog Card Number:
00-102989

Prestel Verlag
Mandlstrasse 26, 80802 Munich, Germany
Tel. +49 (89) 38 17 09-0, Fax +49 (89) 38 17 09-35

4 Bloomsbury Place, London WC1A 2QA
Tel. +44 (20) 7323-5004, Fax +44 (20) 7636-8004

175 Fifth Avenue, Suite 402, New York,
NY 10010
Tel. +1 (212) 995-2720, Fax +1 (212) 995-2733

Prestel books are available worldwide.
Please contact your nearest bookseller or
one of the above Prestel offices for details
concerning your local distributor.

www.prestel.com

Cover design and typography by
Matthias Hauer
Layout by Verlagsservice G. Pfeifer, Germering
Typesetting by EDV-Fotosatz Huber, Germering
Lithography by Repro Line, Munich
Printed by Druckerei Huber, Dießen
Bound by Buchbinderei Monheim
Paper: 150 g/m2 Praximatt

Printed in Germany on acid-free paper

ISBN 3-7913-2176-5

Photo credits

Every effort has been made by the Publisher to
acknowledge all sources and copyright holders.
In the event of any copyright holder being
inadvertently omitted, please contact the
Publisher directly.
    In the catalog section, images are listed by
page number and numbered 1–4 from the top
within their respective column.
l.c. = left-hand column, r.c. = right-hand
column

The Bettmann Archive: 22
Luc Boegly: 87 top, 125 r.c.2
Gero von Boehm: 19
George Cserna: 120 r.c.2, 121 l.c.3, 121 r.c.1, 121
    r.c.2, 121 r.c.3, 122 l.c.3, 123 l.c.3
Robert Damora: 2 bottom, 120 r.c.1, 121 l.c.2
ESTO/Jack Pottle: 126 r.c.1
ESTO/Ezra Stoller: 2 top, 5 top, 120 l.c.1, 121
    l.c.1, 122 l.c.2, 123 l.c.1
Foton Photography/Victor Zbigniew Orlewicz:
    120 l.c.1, 125 r.c.1
Owen Franken: 8 bottom
Serge Hambourg: 8 top, 124 r.c.4
Kiyohiko Higashide: 9
Timothy Hursley: 103 bottom, 125 l.c.3, 125
    r.c.3
Balthazar Korab: 5 bottom, 122 l.c.4, 122 r.c.2
Shang Wei Kouo: 123 l.c.2, 123 l.c.4
Hiroko Koyama/Miho Museum: 125 l.c.4
Robert/Andrea Lautman Photography: 4
Nathaniel Lieberman: 121 r.c.4, 122 l.c.1, 122
    r.c.1, 122 r.c.3, 122 r.c.4, 124 l.c.2, 124 l.c.3,
    124 r.c.1
Hans Namuth/Courtesy of Pei Cobb Freed &
    Partners: 50
Paul Stevenson Oles 78, 81, 83, 91, 125 r.c.4
Rondal Partridge: 3, 121 l.c.4
Richard Payne: 6 top, 123 r.c.3
I.M. Pei: 16, 66, 67, 68, 69, 71, 84, 85, 103 top,
    109, 111
Pei Cobb Freed & Partners: 7, 34, 48, 82, 87
    bottom, 98, 120 l.c.2, 120 r.c.3
Marc Riboud: 124 l.c.1
Steve Rosenthal: 123 r.c.1, 123 r.c.2, 123 r.c.4,
    125 l.c.1
Eric Schiller. 126 l.c.1
Paul Warchol: 6 bottom, 7, 124 l.c.4, 124 r.c.2,
    124 r.c.3, 125 l.c.2